The Words of
JESUS CHRIST

The Words of
JESUS CHRIST

King James Version

◆ BOOK ◆ BLOCKS ◆

This edition first published in 2004 by
Book Blocks an imprint of
CRW Publishing Limited
69 Gloucester Crescent, London NW1 7EG

ISBN 1 904633 25 0

The words are taken from the Authorized
Version of the Bible, as is (with some
minor adaptations) the connecting text.

2 4 6 8 10 9 7 5 3 1

Typeset in Great Britain by Antony Gray
Printed and bound in China by Imago

The Words of
JESUS CHRIST

The first recorded words of Jesus

Luke 2:40–52

WHEN JESUS was twelve years old, strong in spirit and filled with wisdom, and with the grace of God upon him, he went with his parents up to Jerusalem, after the custom of the feast of the Passover.

And when they had fulfilled the days, they set out to return to Nazareth, but the child Jesus tarried behind in Jerusalem; and Joseph and his mother knew not of it, supposing him to have been in the company.

When they had gone a day's journey, they sought him among their kinsfolk and acquaintance, and, finding him not, they turned back to Jerusalem, seeking him.

After three days they found him in the temple, sitting in the midst of the doctors, both hearing them and asking them questions. All that heard him were astonished at his understanding and answers.

His mother said unto him, Son, why hast thou thus dealt with us? Behold thy father and I have sought thee sorrowing.

Jesus replied,

How is it that ye sought me? Wist ye not that I must be about my Father's business?

And they understood not.

He went down with them to Nazareth, and was subject into them: but his mother kept all these sayings in her heart.

And Jesus increased in wisdom and stature, and in favour with God and man.

Jesus is baptized by John

Matthew 3:1–6, 13–17; Mark 1:10–11; Luke 3:22–23

Then Jesus came from Galilee to Jordan unto John, to be baptized of him. But John forbade him, saying, I have need to be baptized of thee, and comest thou to me?

Jesus, answering, said unto him,

Suffer it to be so now: for thus it becometh us to fulfil all righteousness.

Then John suffered him. And Jesus, when he was baptized, went up straightway out of the water: and the heavens were opened unto him and he saw the Spirit of God descending like a dove and lighting upon him; and a voice from heaven was heard saying, This is my beloved Son, in whom I am well pleased. And at this time Jesus was about thirty years of age.

Jesus in the wilderness

Matthew 4:1–11; Mark 1:13; Luke 4:1–13

Then was Jesus led up of the spirit into the wilderness to be tempted by the devil. He was there in the wilderness forty days, and was with the wild beasts. In those days he ate nothing. And when he had fasted forty days and forty nights, he was very hungry. The tempter came: he said, If thou be the Son of God, command that these stones be made bread.

But Jesus answered,

It is written, Man shall not live by bread alone, but by every word that proceedeth out of the mouth of God.

Then, in Jerusalem, the holy city, on a pinnacle of the temple, the devil said unto Jesus, If thou be the Son of God, cast thyself down from hence: for it is written, He shall give his angels charge concerning thee, to keep thee: and in their hands they shall bear thee up, lest at any time thou dash thy foot against a stone.

Jesus answering said,

It is written again, Thou shalt not tempt the Lord thy God.

Again, the devil led Jesus up an exceedingly high mountain, and showed him, in a moment of time, all the kingdoms of the world, and the glory of them, and said to Jesus, All these things will I give thee – all this power, and the glory of them – if thou wilt fall down and worship me; all shall be thine.

And Jesus answered,

Get thee behind me, Satan; get thee hence: for it is written, Thou shalt worship the Lord thy God, and him only shalt thou serve.

Then the devil left him.

Behold the Lamb of God

John 1:19–20, 22–29, 37–51

John, when the Jews sent priests and Levites from Jerusalem to ask him, Who art thou? confessed, I am not the Christ. I am the voice of one crying in the wilderness, Make straight the way of the Lord.

They asked him, Why baptizest thou then, if thou be not that Christ?

John answered, I baptize with water: but there standeth one among you, whom ye know not; he it is, who coming after me is preferred before me, whose shoe's latchet I am not worthy to unloose.

These things were done in Bethabara, beyond Jordan, where John was baptizing.

The next day, John was standing with two of his disciples; and looking upon Jesus as he walked, he said, Behold the Lamb of God, which taketh away the sin of the world.

The two disciples heard John speak, and they followed Jesus.

He saw them following, and said,

What seek ye?

They answered, Rabbi (which is to say, Master), where dwellest thou?

Jesus said,

Come and see.

They came and saw where he dwelt, and they abode with him that day. One of the two was Andrew, Simon Peter's brother. He sought out Simon and said to him, We have found the Messias.

Andrew brought Simon to Jesus. And when Jesus beheld Simon, he said,

Thou art Simon the son of Jona: thou shalt be called Cephas.

Cephas (like Peter), being interpreted, means a rock.

The day following, Jesus went forth into Galilee, and found Philip: he was of Bethsaida, the city of Andrew and Simon Peter. And Jesus said to Philip,

Follow me.

Philip sought out Nathanael and said to him, We have found him of whom Moses did write, Jesus of Nazareth, the son of Joseph.

And Nathanael said, Can there any good thing come out of Nazareth?

Philip said. Come and see.

Jesus saw Nathanael coming, and said,

Behold an Israelite indeed, in whom is no guile!

Nathanael said, Whence knowest thou me?

Jesus answered,

Before that Philip called thee, when thou wast under the fig tree, I saw thee.

Nathanael answered, Master, thou art the Son of God; thou art the King of Israel.

Jesus said,

Because I said unto thee, I saw thee under the fig tree, believest thou? Thou shalt see greater things than these. Verily, verily, I say unto you, hereafter ye shall see heaven open, and the angels of God ascending and descending upon the Son of man.

The Marriage in Cana

John 2:1–11

The third day, there was a marriage in Cana of Galilee. Both Jesus and his disciples were called to the marriage; and the mother of Jesus was there.

When they wanted wine, his mother said to Jesus, They have no wine.

Jesus said,

Woman, what have I to do with thee? Mine hour is not yet come.

His mother told the servants, Whatsoever he saith, do it.

There were set there six waterpots of stone containing two or three firkins apiece.

Jesus said,

Fill the waterpots with water.

They filled them to the brim.

Then he said,

Draw out now, and bear unto the governor of the feast.

And they bear it. The ruler of the feast tasted. The water was made wine. Delighted, he called the bridegroom and said, Every man at the beginning doth set forth good wine; and, when men have well drunk, then that which is worse: but thou hast kept the good wine until now.

This was the beginning of the miracles Jesus did.

The purging of the temple

John 2:12–16, 18–21

The Jews' Passover was at hand: Jesus went up to Jerusalem.

He found in the temple those that sold oxen and sheep and doves; and the changers of money sitting: and when he had made a scourge of small cords, he drove them all out of the temple, and the sheep, and the oxen; and poured out the changers' money and overthrew the tables; and said unto them that sold doves,

Take these things hence; make not my Father's house a house of merchandise.

Then the Jews said unto Jesus, What sign showest thou unto us, seeing that thou doest these things?

He answered,

Destroy this temple, and in three days I will raise it up

Then said the Jews, Forty and six years was this temple in the building, and wilt thou rear it up in three days?

But Jesus spoke of the temple of his body.

Night-time visit

John 3:1–21

A man of the Pharisees. named Nicodemus, a ruler of the Jews, came to Jesus by night, and said unto him, Master, we know that thou art a teacher come from God: for no man can do these miracles that thou doest except God be with him.

Jesus answered,

Verily, verily, I say unto thee, except a man be born again, he cannot see the kingdom of God.

Nicodemus said unto him, How can a man be born when he is old?

Jesus answered,

Verily, verily, I say unto thee, except a man be born of water and of the Spirit, he cannot enter into the kingdom of God. That which is born of the flesh is flesh: and that which is born of the Spirit is spirit.

Marvel not that I said unto thee, Ye must be born again. The wind bloweth where it listeth, and thou hearest the sound thereof but canst not tell whence it cometh and whither it goeth: so is everyone that is born of the Spirit.

Nicodemus said, How can these things be?
Jesus answered,

Art thou a master of Israel, and knowest not these things? Verily, verily, I say unto thee, we speak that we do know, and testify that we have seen; and ye receive not our witness.

If I have told you earthly things and ye believe not, how shall ye believe if I tell you of heavenly things? And no man hath ascended up to heaven but he that came down from heaven, even the Son of man which is in heaven.

And as Moses lifted up the serpent in the wilderness, even so must the Son of man be lifted up: that whosoever believeth in him should not perish, but have eternal life.

For God so loved the world that he gave his only begotten Son, that whosoever believeth in him should not perish but have everlasting life. For God sent not his Son into the world to condemn the world; but that the world through him might be saved.

He that believeth on him is not condemned; but he that believeth not is condemned already, because he hath not believed in the name of the only begotten Son of God.

And this is the condemnation, that light has come into the world, and men loved darkness rather than light, because their deeds were evil. For everyone that doeth evil hateth the light, neither cometh to the light, lest his deeds should be reproved. But he that doeth truth cometh to the light, that his deeds may be made manifest, that they are wrought in God.

A woman of Samaria

John 3:22–28; 4:1–40

After these things came Jesus and his disciples into the land of Judea. John was baptizing in Enon near to Salim. For John was not yet cast into prison.

When Jesus knew how the Pharisees had heard that he made and baptized more disciples than John (though Jesus himself baptized not, but his disciples), he left Judea, and departed again into Galilee. And he must needs go through Samaria.

Then cometh he to a city of Samaria called Sychar, near to the parcel of ground that Jacob gave to his son Joseph.

Now Jacob's well was there. Jesus being wearied with his journey, sat on the well.

There cometh a woman of Samaria to draw water.

Jesus said unto her,

Give me to drink.

The woman replied, How is it that thou, being a Jew, asketh drink of me, a woman of Samaria? For the Jews have no dealings with the Samaritans.

Jesus answered,

If thou knewest the gift of God, and who it is that saith to thee, Give me to drink, thou wouldest have asked of him, and he would have given thee living water.

The woman said, Sir, thou hast nothing to draw with, and the well is deep: from whence then hast thou that living water? Art thou greater than our father Jacob, which gave us the well, and drank thereof himself, and his children, and his cattle?

Jesus said,

Whosoever drinketh of this water shall thirst again; but whosoever drinketh of the water that I shall give him shall never thirst; but the water that I shall give him shall be in him a well of water springing up into everlasting life.

The woman answered, Sir, give me this water, that I thirst not, neither come hither to draw.

Jesus said,

Go, call thy husband, and come hither.

The woman answered, I have no husband.
Jesus said,

Thou hast well said, I have no husband: for thou hast had five husbands; and he whom thou now hast is not thy husband: in that saidst thou truly.

The woman replied, Sir, I perceive that thou art a prophet. Our fathers worshipped in this mountain; and ye say that in Jerusalem is the place where men ought to worship.
Jesus said,

Woman, believe me, the hour cometh when ye shall neither in this mountain, nor yet at Jerusalem, worship the Father. Ye worship ye know not what: we know what we worship, for salvation is of the Jews.

But the hour cometh, and now is, when the true

worshippers shall worship the Father in spirit and in truth: for the Father seeketh such to worship him.

God is a Spirit: and they that worship him must worship him in spirit and in truth.

The woman said, I know that Messias cometh, which is called Christ: when he is come, he will tell us all things.

Jesus said,

I that speak unto thee am he.

The woman went her way into the city and said to the men, Come, see a man which told me all things that ever I did: is not this the Christ?

In the meanwhile his disciples prayed him, saying, Master, eat. But he said,

I have meat to eat that ye know not of.

Therefore said the disciples one to another, Hath any man brought him aught to eat?

Jesus explained to them,

My meat is to do the will of him that sent me, and to finish his work.

Say not ye, There are yet four months, and then cometh harvest? Behold, I say unto you, Lift up your eyes, and look on the fields; for they are white already to harvest. And he that reapeth receiveth wages and gathereth fruit unto life eternal, that both he that soweth and he that reapeth may rejoice together.

And herein is that saying true, One soweth, and another reapeth.

I sent you to reap that whereon ye bestowed no labour: other men laboured, and ye are entered into their labour.

And many of the Samaritans believed on him for the saying of the woman. And many more believed because of his own word.

Christ cures the nobleman's son

John 4:43–53

Jesus came again into Cana of Galilee, where he had made the water wine.

And there was a certain nobleman, whose son was sick at Capernaum. He went unto Jesus, and besought him that he would come down and heal his son: for he was at the point of death.

Then Jesus said to him,

Except ye see signs and wonders, ye will not believe.

The nobleman said, Sir, come down ere my child die.
Jesus answered,

Go thy way: thy son liveth.

The man believed, and went his way And going down, his servants met him and told him, Thy son liveth.

Jesus at the pool of Bethesda; later, he answers the Jews

John 5:1–47

After this there was a feast of the Jews; and Jesus went up to Jerusalem.

At Jerusalem there is a pool, called Bethesda, having five porches. In these lay the blind, halt and withered, waiting for the moving of the water. For an angel went down at a certain season into the pool, and troubled the water: whosoever stepped in first after the troubling of the water was made whole of whatever disease he had.

A certain man was there which had an infirmity thirty and eight years. When Jesus saw him lying there, and knew that he had been now a long time in that state, he said to him,

Wilt thou be made whole?

The afflicted man answered, Sir, I have no man, when the water is troubled, to put me into the pool: while I am coming, another steppeth down before me.

Jesus said to him,

Rise, take up thy bed, and walk.

Immediately the man was made whole, and took up his bed, and walked: and on the same day was the sabbath.

The Jews therefore said unto him that was cured, It is the sabbath day: it is not lawful for thee to carry thy bed.

He answered, He that made me whole, the same said unto me, Take up thy bed, and walk.

Then they asked him, What man is that? And he that was healed wist not who it was: for Jesus had conveyed himself away, a multitude being in that place.

Afterwards Jesus found him in the temple; and said unto him,

Behold, thou art made whole: sin no more, lest a worse thing come unto thee.

The man departed, and told the Jews that it was Jesus which had made him whole And the Jews sought to slay Jesus, because he had done these things on the sabbath day.

But Jesus answered them,

My Father worketh hitherto, and I work.

Then the Jews sought the more to kill him, for saying that God was his father.

Jesus answered the Jews, saying,

Verily, verily, I say unto you, the Son can do nothing of himself but what he seeth the Father do: for what things soever he doeth, these also doeth the Son likewise. For the Father loveth the Son, and showeth him all things that himself doeth: and he will show him greater works than these, that ye may marvel.

For as the Father raiseth up the dead, and quickeneth them, even so the Son quickeneth whom he will.

For the Father judgeth no man but hath committed all judgment unto the Son; that all men should honour the Son, even as they honour the Father. He that honoureth not the Son honoureth not the Father which hath sent him.

Verily, verily, I say unto you, he that heareth my word, and believeth on him that sent me, hath everlasting life, and shall not come unto condemnation; but is passed from death unto life.

Verily, verily, I say unto you, the hour is coming, and now is, when the dead shall hear the voice of the Son of God: and they that hear shall live. For as the Father hath life in himself, so hath he given to the Son to have life in himself; and hath given him authority to execute judgment also because he is the Son of man. Marvel not at this: for the hour is coming in the which all that are in the graves shall hear his voice and shall come forth; they that have done good, unto the resurrection of life; and they that have done evil, unto the resurrection of damnation.

I can of mine own self do nothing: as I hear, I judge: and my judgment is just; because I seek not mine own will, but the will of the Father which hath sent me. If I bear witness of myself, my witness is not true.

There is another that beareth witness of me; and I know that the witness which he witnesseth of me is true.

Ye sent unto John, and he bare witness unto the truth. But I receive not testimony from man: but these things I say, that ye might be saved. He was a burning and a shining light: and ye were willing for a season to rejoice in his light.

But I have greater witness than that of John: for the works which the Father hath given me to finish, the same works that I do, bear witness of me that the Father hath sent me. And the Father himself, which hath sent me, hath borne witness of me. Ye have neither heard his voice at any time, nor seen his shape. And ye have not his word abiding in you: for whom he hath sent, him ye believe not.

Search the scriptures; for in them ye think ye have eternal life: and they are they which testify of me. And ye will not come to me, that ye might have life.

I receive not honour from men. But I know you, that ye have not the love of God in you. I am come in my Father's name, and ye receive me not: if another shall come in his own name, him ye will receive. How can ye believe, which receive honour one of another, and seek not the honour that cometh from God only?

Do not think that I will accuse you to the Father: there is one that accuseth you, even Moses, in whom ye trust. For had ye believed Moses, ye would have believed me: for he wrote of me. But if ye believe not his writings, how shall ye believe my words?

Jesus reads in the synagogue and subsequently begins to preach

Luke 4:16–31; Mark 1:15; Matthew 4:17

Jesus came to Nazareth, where he had been brought up: and, as his custom was, he went into the synagogue on the sabbath day, and stood up to read. When he had opened the book, he read from the place where it was written,

The Spirit of the Lord is upon me, because he hath anointed me to preach the gospel to the poor; he hath sent me to heal the brokenhearted, to preach deliverance to the captives, and recovering of sight to the blind, to set at liberty them that are bruised, to preach the acceptable year of the Lord.

He closed the book, gave it again to the minister, and sat down. The eyes of all them that were in the synagogue were fastened on him: and he told them,

This day is this scripture fulfilled in your ears.

And all bore witness, and wondered at the gracious words which proceeded out of his mouth. They said, Is not this Joseph's son?

And Jesus said,

Ye will surely say unto me this proverb, Physician, heal thyself: whatsoever we have heard done in Capernaum, do also here in thy country. Verily I say unto you, no prophet is accepted in his own country.

But I tell you of a truth, many widows were in Israel in the days of Elias, when the heaven was shut up three years and six months, when great famine was throughout all the land; but unto none of them was Elias sent, save unto Sarepta, a city of Sidon, unto a woman that was a widow.

And many lepers were in Israel in the time of Eliseus the prophet; and none of them was cleansed, saving Naaman the Syrian.

They in the synagogue, when they heard these things, were filled with wrath and rose up and thrust Jesus out, and led him unto the brow of the hill wheron their city was built that they might cast him down headlong.

Now Jesus had heard that John was cast into prison; and, passing through the midst of them, he went his way, departing into Galilee and coming to Capernaum.

Jesus dwelt in Capernaum, preaching the gospel of the kingdom of God, and saying,

The time is fulfilled, and the kingdom of heaven is at hand: repent ye, and believe the gospel. Repent: for the kingdom of God is at hand.

From that time Jesus began to preach; and he taught them on the sabbath days.

Fishers of men

Mark 1:16–26, 35–38; Luke 4:31–38, 44; Matthew 4:17–25

Now as Jesus walked by the sea of Galilee, he saw Simon Peter and Andrew his brother casting a net into the sea: for they were fishers. He said unto them,

Come ye after me, and I will make you to become fishers of men. Follow me.

Straightway they forsook their nets, and followed him.

When he had gone a little farther thence, he saw James the son of Zebedee and John his brother, who were in a ship with their father, mending their nets. He called them: and they left their father in the ship with the hired servants and followed Jesus.

They went into Capernaum; and on the sabbath day Jesus entered into the synagogue, and taught. They were astonished: for his word was with power: he taught them as one that had authority, and not as the scribes.

There was in their synagogue a man with an unclean spirit; and he cried out, Let us alone, thou Jesus of Nazareth. Art thou come to destroy us? I know who thou art: the Holy One of God.

Jesus rebuked him, saying,

Hold thy peace, and come out of him.

When the unclean spirit had thrown the man in the midst, he came out of him, and hurt him not.

Jesus arose and, when they were come out of the synagogue, entered the house of Peter and Andrew, with James and John.

In the morning, rising up a great while before day, Jesus went out into a solitary place, and there prayed.

The people sought him, and came unto him, and stayed him, that he should not depart.

He said,

I must preach the kingdom of God to other cities also: for therefore am I sent.

Simon and they that were with him followed after Jesus, and when they had found him, they said unto him, All men seek for thee.

He answered,

Let us go into the next towns, that I may preach there also: for therefore came I forth.

And Jesus went about all Galilee, teaching in their synagogues, and preaching the gospel of the kingdom. His fame went throughout Syria. And there followed him multitudes from Galilee and Decapolis; from Jerusalem and Judea; and from beyond Jordan.

The Sermon on the Mount

Matthew 5:1–48; 6:1–34; 7:1–29

Seeing the multitudes, Jesus went up into a mountain: and his disciples came unto him: and he taught them, saying,

Blessed are the poor in spirit: for theirs is the kingdom of heaven.

Blessed are they that mourn: for they shall be comforted.

Blessed are the meek: for they shall inherit the earth.

Blessed are they which do hunger and thirst after righteousness: for they shall be filled.

Blessed are the merciful: for they shall obtain mercy.

Blessed are the pure in heart: for they shall see God.

Blessed are the peacemakers: for they shall be called the children of God.

Blessed are they which are persecuted for righteousness' sake: for theirs is the kingdom of heaven.

Blessed are ye, when men shall revile you, and persecute you, and shall say all manner of evil against you falsely, for my sake.

Rejoice, and be exceeding glad: for great is your reward in heaven: for so persecuted they the prophets which were before you.

Ye are the salt of the earth; but if the salt have lost his savour, wherewith shall it be salted? it is thenceforth good for nothing but to be cast out and to be trodden under the feet of men.

Ye are the light of the world. A city that is set on a hill cannot be hid. Neither do men light a candle and put it under a bushel, but on a candlestick; and it giveth light unto all that are in the house. Let your light so shine before men that they may see your good works and glorify your Father which is in heaven.

Think not that I am come to destroy the law, or the prophets: I am not come to destroy, but to fulfil. For verily I say unto you, till heaven and earth pass, one jot or one tittle shall in no wise pass from the law till all be fulfilled.

Whosoever therefore shall break one of these least commandments, and shall teach men so, he shall be called the least in the kingdom of heaven: but whosoever shall do and teach them, the same shall be called great in the kingdom of heaven. For I say unto you that except your righteousness shall exceed the righteousness of the scribes and

Pharisees, ye shall in no case enter into the kingdom of heaven.

Ye have heard that it was said by them of old time, Thou shalt not kill. and whosoever shall kill shall be in danger of the judgment: but I say unto you that whosoever is angry with his brother without a cause shall be in danger of the judgment; and whosoever shall say to his brother, Raca [vain fellow], shall be in danger of the council; but whosoever shall say, Thou fool, shall be in danger of hell fire.

Therefore if thou bring thy gift to the altar, and there rememberest that thy brother hath aught against thee, leave there thy gift before the altar, and go thy way; first be reconciled to thy brother and then come and offer thy gift.

Agree with thine adversary quickly, while thou

art in the way with him, lest at any time the adversary deliver thee to the judge, and the judge deliver thee to the officer, and thou be cast into prison. Verily I say unto thee, thou shalt by no means come out thence till thou hast paid the uttermost farthing.

Ye have heard that it was said by them of old time, Thou shalt not commit adultery: but I say unto you that whosoever looketh on a woman to lust after her hath committed adultery with her already in his heart.

And if thy right eye offend thee, pluck it out, and cast it from thee: for it is profitable for thee that one of thy members should perish, and not that thy whole body should be cast into hell. And if thy right hand offend thee, cut it off, and cast it from thee: for it is profitable for thee that one of thy members *should perish, and not that thy whole body should be cast into hell.*

It hath been said, Whosoever shall put away his wife, let him give her a writing of divorcement: but I say unto you that whosoever shall put away his wife, saving for the cause of fornication, causeth her to commit adultery; and whosoever shall marry her that is divorced committeth adultery.

Again, ye have heard that it hath been said by them of old time, Thou shalt not forswear thyself, but shalt perform unto the Lord thine oaths: but I say unto you, Swear not at all; neither by heaven: for it is God's throne; nor by the earth: for it is his footstool; neither by Jerusalem: for it is the city of the great King. Neither shalt thou swear by thy head, because thou canst not make one hair white or black. But let your communication be, Yea, yea;

Nay, nay: for whatsoever is more than these cometh of evil.

Ye have heard that it hath been said, An eye for an eye, and a tooth for a tooth: but I say unto you that ye resist not evil: but whosoever shall smite thee on thy right cheek, turn to him the other also. And if any man will sue thee at the law, and take away thy coat, let him have thy cloak also. And whosoever shall compel thee to go a mile, go with him twain. Give to him that asketh thee, and from him that would borrow of thee turn not thou away.

Ye have heard that it hath been said, Thou shalt love thy neighbour, and hate thine enemy: but I say unto you, Love your enemies, bless them that curse you, do good to them that hate you, and pray for them which despitefully use you and persecute you, that ye may be the children of your Father which is in heaven: for he maketh his sun to rise on the evil and on the good, and sendeth rain on the just and on the unjust.

For if ye love them which love you, what reward have ye? Do not even the publicans the same? And if ye salute your brethren only, what do ye more than others? Do not even the publicans so?

Be ye therefore perfect, even as your Father, which is in heaven is perfect.

*

Take heed that ye do not your alms before men, to be seen of them; otherwise ye have no reward of your Father which is in heaven.

Therefore when thou doest thine alms, do not sound a trumpet before thee, as the hypocrites do in the synagogues and in the streets, that they may have glory of men. Verily I say unto you, they have *their reward. But when thou doest alms, let not thy left hand know what thy right hand doeth, that thine alms may be in secret: and thy Father which seeth in secret himself shall reward thee openly.*

And when thou prayest, thou shalt not be as the hypocrites are: for they love to pray standing in the synagogues and in the corners of the streets, that they may be seen of men. Verily I say unto you, they have their reward. But thou, when thou prayest, enter into thy closet, and when thou hast shut thy door, pray to thy Father which is in secret; and thy Father which seeth in secret shall reward thee openly.

But when ye pray, use not vain repetitions, as the heathen do: for they think that they shall be heard for their much speaking. Be not ye therefore like unto them, for your Father knoweth what things ye have need of before ye ask him.

After this manner therefore pray ye:

Our Father which art in heaven, hallowed be thy name. Thy kingdom come. Thy will be done in earth, as it is in heaven.

Give us this day our daily bread. And forgive us our debts, as we forgive our debtors.

And lead us not into temptation, but deliver us from evil:

For thine is the kingdom, and the power, and the glory, for ever. Amen.

For if ye forgive men their trespasses, your heavenly Father will also forgive you: but if ye forgive not men their trespasses, neither will your Father forgive your trespasses.

Moreover when ye fast, be not, as the hypocrites, of a sad countenance: for they disfigure their faces that they may appear unto men to fast. Verily I say unto you, they have their reward. But thou, when thou fastest, anoint thy head, and wash thy face, that thou appear not unto men to fast, but unto thy Father which is in secret: and thy Father, which seeth in secret, shall reward thee openly.

Lay not up for yourselves treasures upon earth, where moth and rust doth corrupt, and where thieves break through and steal; but lay up for yourselves treasures in heaven, where neither moth nor rust doth corrupt, and where thieves do not break through nor steal. For where your treasure is, there will your heart be also.

The light of the body is the eye: if therefore thine eye be single, thy whole body shall be full of light. But if thine eye be evil, thy whole body shall be full of darkness. If therefore the light that is in thee be darkness, how great is that darkness!

No man can serve two masters: for either he will hate the one and love the other; or else he will hold to the one and despise the other. Ye cannot serve God and mammon.

Therefore I say unto you, take no thought for your life, what ye shall eat, or what ye shall drink; nor yet for your body, what ye shall put on. Is not the life more than meat, and the body than raiment? Behold the fowls of the air: for they sow not, neither do they reap, nor gather into barns; yet your heavenly Father feedeth them. Are ye not much better than they?

Which of you by taking thought can add one cubic unto his stature? And why take ye thought for raiment? Consider the lilies of the field, how they grow; they toil not, neither do they spin; and yet I say unto you that even Solomon in all his glory was not arrayed like one of these. Wherefore, if God so clothe the grass of the field, which today is, and tomorrow is cast into the oven, shall he not much more clothe you, O ye of little faith?

Therefore take no thought, saying, What shall we eat? or, What shall we drink? or, Wherewithal shall we be clothed? (for after all these things do the Gentiles seek): for your heavenly Father knoweth that ye have need of all these things.

But seek ye first the kingdom of God, and his righteousness, and all these things shall be added unto you. Take therefore no thought for the morrow, for the morrow shall take thought for the things of itself.

Sufficient unto the day is the evil thereof.

*

Judge not, that ye be not judged. For with what judgment ye judge, ye shall be judged: and with what measure ye mete, it shall be measured to you again.

And why beholdest thou the mote that is in thy brother's eye, but considerest not the beam that is in thine own eye? Or how wilt thou say to thy brother, Let me pull out the mote out of thine eye; and, behold, a beam is in thine own eye? Thou hypocrite, first cast out the beam out of thine own eye; and then shalt thou see clearly to cast out the mote out of thy brother's eye.

Give not that which is holy unto the dogs, neither cast ye your pearls before swine, lest they trample them under their feet, and turn again and rend you.

Ask, and it shall be given you; seek, and ye shall find; knock, and it shall be opened unto you: for everyone that asketh receiveth; and he that seeketh findeth; and to him that knocketh it shall be opened.

Or what man is there of you, whom if his son ask bread, will he give him a stone? Or if he ask a fish, will he give him a serpent? If ye then, being evil, know how to give good gifts unto your children, how much more shall your Father which is in heaven give good things to them that ask him?

Therefore all things whatsoever ye would that men should do to you, do ye even so to them: for this is the law and the prophets.

Enter ye in at the strait gate; for wide is the gate, and broad is the way, that leadeth to destruction, and many there be which go in thereat: because strait is the gate, and narrow is the way, which leadeth unto life, and few there be that find it.

Beware of false prophets, which come to you in

sheep's clothing, but inwardly they are ravening wolves. Ye shall know them by their fruits. Do men gather grapes of thorns, or figs of thistles? Even so every good tree bringeth forth good fruit; but a corrupt tree bringeth forth evil fruit. A good tree cannot bring forth evil fruit, neither can a corrupt tree bring forth good fruit. Every tree that bringeth not forth good fruit is hewn down, and cast into the fire. Wherefore by their fruits ye shall know them.

Not every one that saith unto me, Lord, Lord, shall enter into the kingdom of heaven; but he that doeth the will of my Father which is in heaven. Many will say to me in that day, Lord, Lord, have we not prophesied in thy name? and in thy name have cast out devils? and in thy name done many wonderful works? And then will I profess unto them, I never knew you: depart from me, ye that work iniquity.

Therefore whosoever heareth these sayings of mine and doeth them, I will liken him unto a wise man which built his house upon a rock: and the rain descended, and the floods came, and the winds blew and beat upon that house; and it fell not: for it was founded upon a rock.

And everyone that heareth these sayings of mine and doeth them not, he shall be likened unto a foolish man which built his house upon the sand: and the rain descended, and the floods came, and the winds blew and beat upon that house; and it fell: and great was the fall of it.

When Jesus had ended these sayings, the people were astonished at his doctrine: for he taught them as one having authority, and not as the scribes.

A leper cleansed; the draught of fishes; a palsied man cured

Matthew 8:1–4; 9:2–7; Mark 1:40–45; 2:1–12; Luke 5:1–15, 18–25

When Jesus was come down from the mountain, multitudes followed him. And, behold, there came a leper, who, seeing Jesus, besought him, saying, Lord, if thou wilt, thou canst make me clean.

Jesus, moved with compassion, put forth his hand, and touched him, saying,

I will; be thou clean.

And immediately his leprosy was cleansed.
Jesus told him,

See thou tell no man; but go thy way: say nothing to any man. Show thyself to the priest, and offer for thy cleansing those things which Moses commanded, for a testimony unto them.

But he began to blaze abroad the matter, so that the fame of Jesus spread.

It came to pass that, as the people pressed upon Jesus to hear the word of God, he stood by the lake of Gennesaret and saw two ships. He entered into one, which was Simon's, and prayed him that he would thrust out a little from the land. And he sat down, and taught the people out of the ship.

Now when he had finished speaking, he said unto Simon,

Launch out into the deep, and let down your nets for a draught.

Simon answered, Master we have toiled all the night, and have taken nothing: nevertheless, at thy word I will let down the net.

When they had done this, they enclosed such a multitude of fishes that their net broke. They beckoned their partners, which were in the other ship, to come and help them. They came and filled both the ships so full that they began to sink.

When Simon Peter saw it, he fell down at Jesus's knees, saying, Depart from me; for I am a sinful man, O Lord.

For he was astonished at the draught of fishes, as were James and John, which were partners with Simon.

Jesus said unto Simon,

Fear not; from henceforth thou shalt catch men.

When they had brought their ships to land, they forsook all and followed Jesus.

Again Jesus entered into Capernaum after some days; and it was noised that he was in the house. Straightway many were gathered together, insomuch that there was no room to receive them: and he preached the word unto them.

And, behold, men brought one sick of the palsy, lying on a bed borne by four. They could not come nigh unto Jesus for the press: and when they could not find by what way they might bring him in, they went upon the housetop, and uncovered the roof, and let him down through the tiling with his couch into the midst before Jesus.

Jesus seeing their faith said unto the sick of the palsy,

Son, be of good cheer; thy sins be forgiven thee.

Certain of the scribes sitting there, and reasoning in their hearts, said within themselves, This man blasphemeth: who can forgive sins, but God alone?

Jesus knowing their thoughts said,

What reason ye in your hearts? Why reason ye these things? Wherefore think ye evil? Whether is it easier to say to the sick of the palsy, Thy sins be forgiven thee; or to say, Arise, and take up thy bed, and walk? But that ye may know that the Son of man hath power on earth to forgive sins,

He said to the sick of the palsy,

I say unto thee, arise, and take up thy couch, and go thy way into thine house.

And he arose, took up his bed, and departed to his house.

Jesus calls Matthew; he answers his critics with parables

Luke 5:27–39; Matthew 9:9–17; Mark 2:13–22

Jesus went forth again by the sea side, and the multitudes resorted unto him, and he taught them.

As he passed forth from thence, he saw a man named Matthew (Levi, a publican) sitting at the receipt of custom, and he said to him,

Follow me.

And Matthew rose up, left all and followed Jesus.

Later, he made a great feast in his own house, at which many publicans and others sat at meat with Jesus and his disciples.

But the scribes and Pharisees murmured against his disciples, saying, Why do ye eat with publicans and sinners? Why eateth your master with publicans and sinners?

When Jesus heard them he said,

They that are whole need not a physician, but they

that are sick. But go ye and learn what that meaneth. I will have mercy, and not sacrifice: for I am not come to call the righteous, but sinners to repentance.

The disciples of John, who used to fast often, came and said to Jesus, Why do thy disciples fast not?
Jesus replied,

Can ye make the children of the bridechamber fast, while the bridegroom is with them? As long as they have the bridegroom with them, they cannot fast. But the days will come when the bridegroom shall be taken away from them, and then shall they fast in those days.

He spoke to them in parables:

No man seweth a piece of new cloth upon an old garment, else the new piece that filleth it up agreeth not with the old: it taketh away from the old, and the rent is made worse.

And no man putteth new wine into old bottles: else the bottles will be marred: the new wine will burst the bottles, and be spilled, and the bottles shall perish. But new wine must be put into new bottles; and both are preserved.

No man having drunk old wine straightway desireth new; for he says, The old is better.

Jesus challenged on uses of the sabbath; he ordains his apostles and confounds the scribes

Matthew 12:1–16; Mark 2:23–28; 3:1–15, 22–29:
Luke 6:1–13; 11:24–26

At that time Jesus went on the sabbath day through the cornfields; and his disciples were hungry and began, as they went, to pluck the ears of corn and to eat, rubbing them with their hands.

But certain of the Pharisees said unto Jesus, Behold, why do thy disciples on the sabbath day that which is not lawful?

Jesus said unto them,

Have ye never read so much as this: what David did, when himself was an hungred, and had need, he, and they which were with him: how he went into the house of God in the days of Abiathar the high priest, and did take and eat the shewbread, and gave also to them which were with him, which was not lawful for him to eat, neither for them which were with him, but for the priests alone?

Or have ye not read in the law, how that on the sabbath days the priests in the temple profane the sabbath, and are blameless?

But I say unto you that in this place is one greater than the temple. But if ye had known what this meaneth – I will have mercy, and not sacrifice – ye would not have condemned the guiltless.

The sabbath was made for man, and not man for the sabbath: therefore the Son of man is Lord even of the sabbath day.

On another sabbath, Jesus entered into the synagogue and taught.

There was a man there whose right hand was withered. The scribes and Pharisees watched Jesus, whether he would heal on the sabbath day.

But he knew their thoughts, and he said to the man,

Rise up, and stand forth in the midst.

He arose and stood forth.
Then said Jesus unto them,

I will ask you one thing: Is it lawful on the sabbath days to do good, or to do evil? to save life, or to kill? to save life, or to destroy it?

But they held their peace.
And Jesus said,

What man shall there be among you that shall have one sheep, and if it fall into a pit on the sabbath day, will he not lay hold on it, and lift it out? How much then is a man better than a sheep? Wherefore it is lawful to do well on the sabbath days.

When Jesus had looked round about on them with anger, being grieved for the hardness of their hearts, he said to the man,

Stretch forth thine hand.

He did so: and his hand was restored whole, like as the other.

The Pharisees were filled with madness; they went forth, and straightaway took counsel with the Herodians what they might do to Jesus.

Jesus knew it: he withdrew himself with his disciples to the sea. And he straitly charged them that they should not make him known.

Jesus goeth up into a mountain, and calleth unto him whom he would: and they came. He ordained twelve, whom also he named apostles, that they should be with him, and that he might send them forth to preach, and to have power to heal sicknesses, and to cast out devils.

The scribes said, He hath Beelzebub, and by the prince of devils casteth he out devils.

Jesus said unto them in parables,:

How can Satan cast out Satan?

And if a kingdom be divided against itself, that kingdom cannot stand. And if a house be divided against itself, that house cannot stand. And if Satan rise up against himself, and be divided, he cannot stand, but hath an end.

No man can enter into a strong man's house, and spoil his goods, except he will first bind the strong man; and then he will spoil his house.

Verily I say unto you, all sins shall be forgiven unto the sons of men, and blasphemies wheresoever they shall blaspheme; but he that shall blaspheme against the Holy Ghost hath never forgiveness, but is in danger of eternal damnation, because he hath an unclean spirit.

When the unclean spirit is gone out of a man, he walketh through dry places, seeking rest: and finding none, he saith, I will return unto my house whence I came out. And when he cometh, he findeth it swept and garnished. Then goeth he, and taketh to him seven other spirits more wicked than himself; and the last state of that man is worse than the first.

The sermon in the plain

Matthew 10:2–4; Mark 3:16–19; Luke 6:14–49

In those days Jesus went out into a mountain, and continued all night in prayer to God. When it was day, he came with his twelve disciples and stood in the plain; and a multitude of people out of all Judea and Jerusalem and from the sea coast of Tyre and Sidon came to hear him, and to be healed.

Jesus lifted up his eyes on his disciples, and said,

Blessed be ye poor: for yours is the kingdom of God.

Blessed are ye that hunger now: for ye shall be filled.

Blessed are ye that weep now: for ye shall laugh.

Blessed are ye, when men shall hate you, and when they shall separate you from their company, and shall reproach you, and cast out your name as evil, for the Son of man's sake.

Rejoice ye in that day and leap for joy: for, behold, your reward is great in heaven: for in the like manner did their fathers unto the prophets.

But woe unto you that are rich! for ye have received your consolation.

Woe unto you that are full! for ye shall hunger.

Woe unto you that laugh now! for ye shall mourn and weep.

Woe unto you, when all men shall speak well of you! for so did their fathers to the false prophets.

But I say unto you which hear: Love your enemies, do good to them which hate you, bless them that curse you and pray for them which despitefully use you.

And unto him that smiteth thee on the one cheek offer also the other; and him that taketh away thy cloak forbid not to take thy coat also.

Give to every man that asketh of thee; and of him that taketh away thy goods ask them not again.

And as ye would that men should do to you, do ye also to them likewise .

For if ye love them which love you, what thanks have ye? for sinners also love those that love them. And if ye do good to them which do good to you, what thanks have ye? for sinners also do even the same.

And if ye lend to them of whom ye hope to receive, what thanks have ye? for sinners also lend to sinners, to receive as much again.

But love ye your enemies, and do good, and lend, hoping for nothing again; and your reward shall be great, and ye shall be the children of the Highest: for he is kind unto the unthankful and to the evil.

Be ye therefore merciful, as your Father also is merciful.

Judge not, and ye shall not be judged; condemn not, and ye shall not be condemned; forgive, and ye shall be forgiven.

Give, and it shall be given unto you; good measure, pressed down, and shaken together, and running over, shall men give into your bosom. For with the same measure that ye mete withal it shall be measured to you again.

And he spake a parable unto them,

Can the blind lead the blind? shall they not both fall into the ditch? The disciple is not above his master: but everyone that is perfect shall be as his master.

And why beholdest thou the mote that is in thy brother's eye, but perceivest not the beam that is in thine own eye? Either how canst thou say to thy brother, Brother, let me pull out the mote that is in thine eye, when thou thyself beholdest not the beam that is in thine own eye? Thou hypocrite, cast first the beam out of thine own eye, and then shalt thou see clearly to pull out the mote that is in thy brother's eye.

For a good tree bringeth not forth corrupt fruit; neither doth a corrupt tree bring forth good fruit. For every tree is known by his own fruit. For of thorns men do not gather figs, nor of a bramble bush gather they grapes.

A good man out of the good treasure of his heart bringeth forth that which is good; and an evil man out of the evil treasure of his heart bringeth forth that which is evil: for of the abundance of the heart the mouth speaketh.

And why call ye me, Lord, Lord, and do not the things which I say? Whosoever cometh to me, and heareth my sayings, and doeth them, I will show you to whom he is like: he is like a man which built a house, and dug deep, and laid the foundation on a rock: and when the flood arose, the stream beat vehemently upon that house, and could not shake it: for it was founded upon a rock. But he that heareth, and doeth not, is like a man that without a foundation built a house upon the earth; against which the stream did beat vehemently, and immediately it fell; and the ruin of that house was great.

The centurion's servant healed

Matthew 8:5–13; Luke 7:1–18

When Jesus was entered into Capernaum, there came unto him a centurion beseeching him, saying, Lord, my servant lieth at home sick of the palsy, grievously tormented.

The elders of the Jews came and pleaded on his behalf, saying that he was worthy – For he loveth our nation, and hath built us a synagogue.

And Jesus said to the centurion,

I will come and heal him.

The centurion answered, Lord, I am not worthy that thou shouldest come under my roof: but speak the word only, and my servant shall be healed.

Jesus marvelled, and turned and said to the people that followed him,

Verily I say unto you, I have not found so great faith, no, not in Israel. And I say unto you that

many shall come from the east and west, and shall sit down with Abraham, and Isaac, and Jacob, in the kingdom of heaven; but the children of the kingdom shall be cast out into outer darkness: there shall be weeping and gnashing of teeth.

And Jesus said unto the centurion,

Go thy way; and as thou hast believed, so be it done unto thee.

His servant was healed in the selfsame hour.

The day after, Jesus went into a city called Nain: many of his disciples and a crowd of people went with him.

Now when he came nigh to the gate of the city, behold, there was a dead man carried out, the only son of a widow; and many people of the city were with her. The Lord had compassion on her, and said,

Weep not.

He touched the bier and said,

Young man, I say unto thee, Arise.

And he that was dead sat up, and began to speak.

There came a fear on all: they glorified God, saying, A great prophet is risen among us.

This rumour of Jesus went forth throughout all Judea and the region round about. And the disciples of John the Baptist brought him news of all these things.

Concerning John the Baptist

Matthew 11:2–15, 16–19; Luke 7:24–35

Now when John had heard in the prison the works of Christ, he sent two of his disciples to Jesus. Unto him they said, John Baptist hath sent us unto thee, saying, Art thou he that should come? or do we look for another?

And in that same hour Jesus cured many people of their infirmities; and unto many that were blind he gave sight.

Then said Jesus unto the two disciples,

Go your way, and tell John what things ye have seen and heard: how the blind receive their sight, and the lame walk, the lepers are cleansed, and the deaf hear, the dead are raised up, and the poor have the gospel preached to them. And blessed is he, whosoever shall not be offended in me.

When the messengers of John were departed, Jesus began to speak unto the people concerning John,

What went ye out into the wilderness for to see? A reed shaken with the wind? But what went ye out for to see? A man clothed in soft raiment? Behold, they that wear soft clothing, they which are gorgeously apparelled and live delicately, are in kings' courts, in kings' houses.

But what went ye out for to see? A prophet? Yea, I say unto you, and much more than a prophet. For this is he of whom it is written, Behold, I send my messenger before thy face, which shall prepare thy way before thee.

Verily, I say unto you, among them that are born of women there hath not risen a greater prophet than John the Baptist: notwithstanding, he that is least in the kingdom of God is greater than he.

And from the days of John the Baptist until now the kingdom of heaven suffereth violence, and the violent take it by force. For all the prophets and the law prophesied until John. And if ye will receive it, this is Elias, which was for to come.

He that hath ears to hear, let him hear.

The people that heard him, and the publicans, justified God, being baptized with the baptism of John. But the Pharisees and lawyers rejected the counsel of God against themselves, being not baptized of him.

Jesus said,

But whereunto then shall I liken the men of this generation? and to what are they like? They are like unto children sitting in the marketplace and calling unto their fellows, one to another, and saying, We have piped unto you, and ye have not danced; we have mourned unto you, and ye have not lamented: ye have not wept.

For John the Baptist came neither eating bread

nor drinking wine; and they say, He hath a devil. The Son of man is come eating and drinking; and they say, Behold a man gluttonous and a winebibber, a friend of publicans and sinners!

But wisdom is justified of all her children.

Woe unto those cities that fail to repent

Matthew 11:20–30; Luke 10:13–15

Then began he to upbraid the cities wherein most of his mighty works were done, because they repented not:

Woe unto thee, Chorazin! woe unto thee, Bethsaida! for if the mighty works, which were done in you, had been done in Tyre and Sidon, they would have repented long ago in sackcloth and ashes. But I say unto you, it shall be more tolerable for Tyre and Sidon at the day of judgment, than for you.

And thou, Capernaum, which are exalted unto heaven, shall be brought down to hell: for if the mighty works, which have been done in thee, had been done in Sodom, it would have remained until this day. But I say unto you that it shall be more tolerable for the land of Sodom in the day of judgment than for thee.

And Jesus went on to say,

I thank thee, O Father, Lord of heaven and earth, because thou hast hid these things from the wise and prudent, and hast revealed them unto babes. Even so, Father: for so it seemed good in thy sight.

All things are delivered unto me of my Father, and no man knoweth the Son, but the Father; neither knoweth any man the Father, save the Son, and he whomsoever the Son will reveal him.

Come unto me, all ye that labour and are heavy laden, and I will give you rest.

Take my yoke upon you and learn of me; for I am meek and lowly in heart: and ye shall find rest unto your souls. For my yoke is easy, and my burden is light.

The woman with the alabaster box of ointment

Luke 7:36–50

Simon, one of the Pharisees, desired that Jesus would eat with him. And Jesus went into his house, and sat down to meat.

And, behold, a woman in the city, which was a sinner, when she knew that Jesus sat at meat in the Pharisee's house, brought an alabaster box of ointment, and stood behind him weeping; then she began to wash Jesus's feet with tears, and did wipe them with the hairs of her head, and kissed his feet, and anointed them with the ointment.

Now the Pharisee spake within himself, saying, This man, if he were a prophet, would have known what manner of woman this is; for she is a sinner.

Jesus said unto him,

Simon, I have somewhat to say unto thee: there was a certain creditor which had two debtors; the one owed five hundred pence, and the other fifty.

And when they had nothing to pay, he frankly forgave them both. Tell me therefore, which of them will love him most?

Simon answered, I suppose it will be he to whom he forgave most.

Jesus said,

Thou hast rightly judged.

He turned to the woman, and said unto Simon,

Seest thou this woman?

I entered into thine house and thou gavest me no water for my feet: but she hath washed my feet with tears, and wiped them with the hairs of her head.

Thou gavest me no kiss: but this woman, since the time I came in, hath not ceased to kiss my feet.

My head with oil thou didst not anoint: but this woman hath anointed my feet with ointment.

Wherefore I say unto thee, her sins, which are many, are forgiven; for she loveth much: but to whom little is forgiven, the same loveth little.

And he said unto her,

Thy sins are forgiven.

They that sat at meat with him began to say within themselves, Who is this that forgiveth sins also?
Jesus said to the woman,

Thy faith hath saved thee; go in peace.

Jesus restores sight and speech to one possessed, and admonishes the Pharisees

Matthew 12:22–37; Luke 11:17–23; Mark 3:22–29

Unto Jesus was brought one possessed with a devil, blind and dumb; and he healed him, insomuch that the blind and dumb man both spake and saw.

The people were amazed, and said, Is not this the son of David? But the Pharisees said, This fellow doth not cast out devils without the help of Beelzebub the prince of the devils.

Jesus knew their thoughts, and said unto them,

Every kingdom divided against itself is brought to desolation; and every city or house divided against itself falleth: it shall not stand; and if Satan cast out Satan, he is divided against himself; how shall then his kingdom stand – because ye say that I cast out devils through Beelzebub?

And if I by Beelzebub cast out devils, by whom do your children cast them out? Therefore they shall be your judges.

But if I with the finger of God cast out devils by the Spirit of God, no doubt then the kingdom of God is come unto you.

Or else, how can one enter into a strong man's house, and spoil his goods, except he first bind the strong man? and then he will spoil his house.

When a strong man is armed and keepeth his palace, his goods are in peace; but when a stronger than he shall come upon him, and overcome him, he taketh from him all his armour, wherein he trusted, and divideth the spoils.

He that is not with me is against me; and he that gathereth not with me scattereth abroad.

Wherefore I say unto you, all manner of sin and

blasphemy shall be forgiven unto the sons of men: but the blasphemy against the Holy Ghost shall not be forgiven unto men.

And whosoever speaketh a word against the Son of man, it shall be forgiven him; but whosoever speaketh against the Holy Ghost is in danger of eternal damnation: it shall not be forgiven him, neither in this world, neither in the world to come.

Either make the tree good, and his fruit good; or else make the tree corrupt: for the tree is known by his fruit.

O generation of vipers, how can ye, being evil, speak good things? for out of the abundance of the heart the mouth speaketh. A good man out of the good treasure of the heart bringeth forth good things: and an evil man out of the evil treasure bringeth forth evil things.

But I say unto you that every idle word that men shall speak, they shall give account thereof in the day of judgment.

For by thy words thou shalt be justified, and by thy words thou shalt be condemned.

Jesus answers those who seek a sign

Matthew 12:38–45

Certain of the scribes and of the Pharisees answered Jesus, saying, Master, we would see a sign from thee.

But he said unto them,

An evil and adulterous generation seeketh after a sign; and there shall no sign be given to it, but the sign of the prophet Jonas: for as Jonas was three days and three nights in the whale's belly, so shall the Son of man be three days and three nights in the heart of the earth.

The men of Nineveh shall rise in judgment with this generation, and shall condemn it: because they repented at the preaching of Jonas; and, behold, a greater than Jonas is here.

The queen of the south shall rise up in the

judgment with this generation, and shall condemn it: for she came from the uttermost parts of the earth to hear the wisdom of Solomon; and, behold, a greater than Solomon is here.

When the unclean spirit is gone out of a man, he walketh through dry places, seeking rest, and findeth none. Then he saith, I will return into my house from whence I came out; and when he is come, he findeth it empty, swept and garnished. Then goeth he, and taketh with himself seven other spirits more wicked than himself, and they enter in and dwell there: and the last state of that man is worse than the first. Even so shall it be also unto this wicked generation.

Jesus speaks of his mother and his brethren and teaches in parables

Matthew 12:46–50; 13:1–30; Mark 3:31–35; 4:1–29;
Luke 8:4–18, 19–21

While Jesus yet talked, behold, there came his mother and his brethren, desiring to speak with him, but they could not get near him for the press. Then one said unto him, Thy mother and thy brethren without seek for thee.

But Jesus answered him that told him,

Who is my mother? and who are my brethren?

He looked on them which sat about him, stretched forth his hand towards his disciples, and said,

Behold my mother and my brethren! My mother and my brethren are these which hear the word of God, and do it. For whosoever shall do the will of God my Father which is in heaven, the same is my brother, and my sister, and mother.

The same day Jesus went out of the house and sat by the sea side. A great many people were come to him out of every city, so he entered into a ship and sat a little out to sea. The multitude stood on the shore. And Jesus spake many things unto them in parables, saying,

Hearken. Behold, a sower went forth to sow his seed: and it came to pass, as he sowed, some fell by the wayside, and it was trodden down, and the fowls of the air came and devoured it up.

Some seed fell on stony ground where it had not much earth: and immediately it sprang up, because it had not much deepness of earth: but when the sun was up, because it had no depth of earth, it was scorched; and because it had no root, it withered away.

And some seed fell upon a rock: as soon as it was sprung up, it withered away, because it lacked moisture.

And some fell among thorns, and the thorns grew up with it, and choked it, and it yielded no fruit.

But other seed fell into good ground, and did yield fruit: that sprang up, and increased, and bare fruit, some a hundredfold, some sixtyfold and some thirtyfold.

He that hath ears to hear, let him hear.

When he was alone, his disciples came and said unto Jesus, Why speakest thou in parables?

He answered,

Because it is given unto you to know the mysteries of the kingdom of heaven, but to them it is not given but in parables: unto them that are without, all these things are done in parables.

For whosoever hath, to him shall be given, and he shall have more abundance: but whosoever hath not, from him shall be taken away even that he hath.

Therefore speak I to them in parables: because they seeing see not; and hearing they hear not; neither do they understand.

And in them is fulfilled the prophecy of Esaias, which saith, By hearing ye shall hear, and shall not understand, and seeing ye shall see and shall not perceive: for this people's heart is waxed gross, and their ears are dull of hearing, and their eyes they have closed; lest at any time they should see with their eyes, and hear with their ears, and should understand with their heart, and should be converted, and I should heal them, and their sins should be forgiven them.

But blessed are your eyes, for they see: and your ears, for they hear. For verily I say unto you that many prophets and righteous men have desired to see those things which ye see, and have not seen them; and to hear those things which ye hear, and have not heard them.

And he asked them,

Know ye not this parable? And how then will ye know all parables?

Hear ye therefore the parable of the sower. Now the parable is this:

The seed is the word of God. The sower soweth the word. When anyone heareth the word of the kingdom, and understandeth it not, then cometh immediately Satan the wicked one, and catcheth away that word, which was sown in his heart: the devil taketh away the word out of their hearts, lest they should believe and be saved. This is he which received seed by the wayside, where the word is sown.

They on the rock received seed into stony places: these are they who when they have heard the word, anon with joy receive it, and for a while believe; yet have no root in themselves, and so endure but for a time; and in time of temptation fall away: for afterward, when affliction or tribulation or persecution ariseth for the word's sake, immediately they are offended.

And they which received the seed among thorns are they which, when they have heard the word, go forth and are choked with the cares of this world and the deceitfulness of riches and the pleasures of this life; and bring no fruit to perfection: the lusts of other things entering in, choke the word, and it becometh unfruitful.

But he that received the seed into the good ground is he that in an honest and good heart, having

heard the word, understandeth it, and keepeth it,
and beareth fruit with patience, and bringeth forth
some a hundredfold, some sixty, some thirty.

Another parable put he forth unto them, saying,

The kingdom of heaven is likened unto a man
which sowed good seed in his field: but while men
slept, his enemy came and sowed tares among the
wheat, and went his way. But when the blade was
sprung up, and brought forth fruit, then appeared
the tares also.

So the servants of the householder came and said
unto him, Sir, didst not thou sow good seed in thy
field? from whence then hath it tares?

He said unto them, An enemy hath done this.

The servants said unto him, Wilt thou then that
we go and gather them up?

But he said, Nay; lest while ye gather up the tares, ye root up also the wheat with them. Let both grow together until the harvest: and in the time of harvest I will say to the reapers, Gather ye together first the tares, and bind them in bundles to burn them: but gather the wheat into my barn.

And he said unto them, Is a candle brought to be put under a bushel or under a bed? and not to be set on a candlestick?

No man, when he hath lighted a candle, covereth it with a vessel, or putteth it under a bed, but setteth it on a candlestick, that they which enter in may see the light.

For there is nothing hid, which shall not be manifested; neither was anything kept secret, but that it should be known and come abroad.

If any man have ears to hear, let him hear.

Take heed what ye hear: with what measure ye mete, it shall be measured to you; and unto you that hear shall more be given. For he that hath, to him shall be given; and he that hath not, from him shall be taken even that which he hath.

And he went on to say,

So is the kingdom of God as if a man should cast seed into the ground; and should sleep and rise, night and day, and the seed should spring and grow up, he knoweth not how. For the earth bringeth forth fruit of herself; first the blade, then the ear, after that the full corn in the ear. But when the fruit is brought forth, immediately he putteth in the sickle, because the harvest is come.

Parables

Mark 4:30–34,35–41; Matthew 13:31–34, 36–52;
Luke 13:18–21; 8:22–25

Another parable put he forth unto them, saying,

Whereunto shall we liken the kingdom of God? or with what comparison shall we compare it? A grain of mustard seed is the least of all seeds: is indeed less than all the seeds that be in the earth; but when it is sown in the earth, it groweth up: it becometh greater than all herbs; it shooteth out great branches, and becometh a tree, so that the fowls of the air come and lodge in the branches thereof.

Then said he,

Unto what is the kingdom of God like? and

whereunto shall I resemble it? The kingdom of heaven is like unto a grain of mustard seed, which a man took and cast into a garden in his field; and it grew, and waxed a great tree, and the birds of the air lodged in the branches thereof, in the shadow of it.

Again Jesus said,

Whereunto shall I liken the kingdom of God? The kingdom of heaven is like unto leaven, which a woman took, and hid in three measures of meal, till the whole was leavened.

All these things spake Jesus unto the multitude in parables.

Then he sent the multitude away, and went into the house: and his disciples came, saying, Declare unto us the parable of the tares of the field.

He answered,

He that soweth the good seed is the Son of man; the field is the world; the good seed are the children of the kingdom; but the tares are the children of the wicked one; the enemy that sowed them is the devil; the harvest is the end of the world; and the reapers are the angels.

As therefore the tares are gathered and burned in the fire, so shall it be in the end of this world. The Son of man shall send forth his angels, and they shall gather out of his kingdom all things that offend, and them which do iniquity; and shall cast them into a furnace of fire: there shall be wailing and gnashing of teeth.

Then shall the righteous shine forth as the sun in the kingdom of their Father.

Who hath ears to hear, let him hear.

Again, the kingdom of heaven is like unto a treasure hid in a field; the which when a man hath found, he hideth, and for joy thereof goeth and selleth all that he hath, and buyeth that field.

Again, the kingdom of heaven is like unto a merchantman, seeking goodly pearls: who, when he had found one pearl of great price, went and sold all that he had, and bought it.

Again, the kingdom of heaven is like unto a net, that was cast into the sea, and gathered of every kind: which, when it was full, they drew to shore, and sat down, and gathered the good into vessels, but cast the bad away.

So shall it be at the end of the world: the angels shall come forth, and sever the wicked from the just, and shall cast them into the furnace of fire: there shall be wailing and gnashing of teeth.

Jesus asked them,

Have ye understood all these things?

They replied, Yea, Lord.
Then said he unto them,

Therefore every scribe which is instructed unto the kingdom of heaven is like unto a man that is a householder, which bringeth forth out of his treasure things new and old.

And with many such parables spake Jesus the word unto them as were able to hear it.

The same day, when even was come, Jesus entered into a ship. His disciples followed, and he said unto them,

Let us pass over unto the other side of the lake.

As they sailed, the waves beat into the ship to such an extent that the ship was covered with the waves.

Jesus was in the hinder part of the ship, asleep on a pillow: and his disciples awoke him, saying, Lord, save us: we perish.

He said unto them,

Why are ye fearful, O ye of little faith?

Then he arose and rebuked the winds, and the raging of the water: he said unto the sea,

Peace, be still.

The wind ceased: there was a great calm, and Jesus said unto his disciples,

Why are ye fearful? where is your faith? how is it that ye have no faith?

But the men marvelled, saying, What manner of man is this, that even the winds and the sea obey him?

The madman and the swine

Mark 5:1–20; Luke 8:26–40; Matthew 8:28–34

They came over the sea and arrived at the country of the Gadarenes, over against Galilee.

And when Jesus was come out of the ship, immediately there met him out of the tombs a man with an unclean spirit, who wore no clothes, neither abode in any house but among the tombs: he had been long afflicted, and no man could bind him, not even with chains.

Jesus said,

Come out of the man, thou unclean spirit.

He fell down before Jesus, and cried out, What have I to do with thee, Jesus, thou Son of God most high? I beseech thee, torment me not.

And Jesus asked him,

What is thy name?

Because many devils were entered into him, he replied, Legion: for we are many.

Now there was a good way off from them a herd of swine feeding. And the devils besought Jesus, saying, If thou cast us out, suffer us to go away into the herd of swine.

Jesus agreed and said,

Go.

The unclean spirits went out, and entered into the swine; and the herd ran violently down a steep place into the sea, and perished in the waters. They were about two thousand.

They that fed the swine went and told it in the city. And, behold, the whole city came out: but when they saw the man sitting at the feet of Jesus, clothed, and in his right mind, the Gadarenes were afraid and besought Jesus to depart out of their coasts.

Jesus went up into the ship.

Now the man, out of whom the devils were departed, besought Jesus that he might be with him: but Jesus sent him away, saying,

Return to thine own house. Go home to thy friends; tell them how the Lord had compassion on thee,

*and show them how great things God hath done
unto thee.*

Jesus passed over by ship unto the other side, and came into
his own city, where he was gladly received.

Jairus's daughter healed

Luke 9:41–42, 49–56, 43–48; Mark 5:22–24, 35–43,25–34;
Matthew 9:18–19, 23–26, 27–30

And, behold, there came one of the rulers of the synagogue, a man named Jairus. He fell at Jesus's feet and he besought Jesus that he would come to his house, saying, My little daughter lieth at the point of death: I pray thee, come and lay thy hands on her and she shall live.

She was of the age of twelve years and was his only daughter.

Jesus arose and followed him, and so did his disciples, and many people thronged about him.

There cometh one from the ruler's house, saying to Jairus, Thy daughter is dead: why troublest thou the Master further?

Jesus heard. He said,

Be not afraid, only believe. Fear not, believe only, and she shall be made whole.

Jesus came to Jairus's house, and saw the tumult: the minstrels making a noise, and them that wept.

He suffered no man to go in, save Peter, James and John, and the father and the mother of the maiden. All wept, and bewailed her.

When Jesus was come in, he saith unto them,

Why make ye this ado, and weep? Weep not. Give place. The damsel is not dead, but sleepeth.

They laughed him to scorn, knowing that she was dead.

He put them all out.

Jesus, and the father and mother of the damsel, and they that were with them, entered in where the maiden was lying.

He took her by the hand, saying,

Maid, arise.

She arose straightway, and walked. Jesus commanded that something be given her to eat.

Behold a certain woman, which was diseased twelve years, and had suffered many things from many physicians, and had spent all that she had, and was nothing bettered, but rather grew worse: she came in the press behind, and touched the hem of

Jesus's garment: for she said within herself, If I may but touch his clothes, I shall be whole.

Straightway she felt in her body that she was healed.

Jesus, knowing that virtue had gone out of him, turned him about in the press, and said,

Who touched me?

When all denied, Peter said, Master, the multitude throng thee and press thee, and sayest thou, Who touched me?

Jesus said,

Somebody hath touched me: for I perceive that virtue is gone out of me. Who touched my clothes?

He looked about to see her that had done this thing. The woman fearing and trembling, knowing what was done in her, came and told him the truth, before all the people: for what cause she had touched him, and how she was healed immediately.

Jesus said unto her,

Daughter, be of good comfort; thy faith hath made thee whole. Go in peace, and be whole of thy plague.

When Jesus departed thence, two blind men followed him, crying, Thou Son of David, have mercy on us.

When he was come into the house, the blind men came to him: and Jesus asked them,

Believe ye that I am able to do this?

They said, Yea, Lord.
Then touched he their eyes, saying,

According to your faith be it unto you.

And their eyes were opened.
Jesus straitly charged them,

See that no man know it.

But they spread abroad his fame in all that country.

Jesus finds himself without honour in his own country; he instructs his apostles

Mark 6:1–6, 7–13; Matthew 13:54–58; 9:35–38; 10:5–42; Luke 9:1–6

Jesus went out from thence, and came into his own country. When the sabbath day was come, he began to teach in the synagogue: and many hearing him were astonished, saying, What wisdom is this which is given unto him? Is not this the carpenter, the son of Joseph? Is not his mother called Mary? and his brethren, James, and Joses, and Simon, and Judas? And his sisters, are they not all here? Whence then has this man all this wisdom? And they were offended.

But Jesus said unto them,

A prophet is not without honour, save in his own country, and among his own kin, and in his own house.

And he did not many works there, because of their unbelief.

Jesus went about the cities and villages, preaching the gospel of the kingdom and healing sickness among the people.

But when he saw the multitudes, he was moved with compassion, because they fainted and were scattered abroad, as sheep having no shepherd. Then saith he to his disciples,

The harvest truly is plenteous, but the labourers are few; pray ye therefore the Lord of the harvest, that he will send forth labourers into his harvest.

Jesus called unto him the twelve, and began to send them forth by two and two; and gave them power over unclean spirits, and to cure diseases.

These twelve Jesus sent forth to preach the gospel of the kingdom; and he commanded them:

Go not into the way of the Gentiles, and into any city of the Samaritans enter ye not; but go rather to the lost sheep of the house of Israel. And as ye go, preach, saying, The kingdom of heaven is at hand.

Heal the sick, cleanse the lepers, raise the dead, cast out devils: freely ye have received, freely give.

Take nothing for your journey, neither staves nor bread; provide neither gold, nor silver, nor brass in your purses, nor scrip for your journey, neither two coats apiece; nor yet shoes, but be shod with sandals; for the workman is worthy of his meat.

And into whatsoever city or town ye shall enter, in what place soever ye enter, enquire who in it is worthy, and there abide till ye thence depart. And when ye come into a house, salute it. And if the house be worthy, let your peace come upon it; but if it be not worthy, let your peace return to you. And whosoever shall not receive you, nor hear your words, when ye depart out of that house or city, shake off the very dust from your feet for a testimony against them. Verily I say unto you, it shall be more tolerable for the land of Sodom and Gomorrah in the day of judgment than for that city.

Behold, I send you forth as sheep in the midst of wolves: be ye therefore wise as serpents, and harmless as doves.

But beware of men: for they will deliver you up to the councils, and they will scourge you in their synagogues; and ye shall be brought before governors and kings for my sake, for a testimony against them and the Gentiles.

But when they deliver you up, take no thought how or what ye shall speak: for it shall be given you in that same hour what ye shall speak. For it is not ye that speak, but the Spirit of your Father which speaketh in you.

And the brother shall deliver up the brother to death, and the father the child; and the children shall rise up against their parents, and cause them to be put to death.

And ye shall be hated of all men for my name's sake: but he that endureth to the end shall be saved. But when they persecute you in this city, flee ye into another: for verily I say unto you, Ye shall not have gone over the cities of Israel, till the Son of man be come.

The disciple is not above his master, nor the servant above his lord. It is enough for the disciple that he be as his master, and the servant as his lord. If they have called the master of the house Beelzebub, how much more shall they call them of his household?

Fear them not therefore: for there is nothing covered that shall not be revealed; and hid that shall not be known. What I tell you in darkness *that speak ye in light: and what ye hear in the ear, that preach ye upon the housetops. And fear not them which kill the body, but are not able to kill the soul: but rather fear him which is able to destroy both soul and body in hell.*

Are not two sparrows sold for a farthing? and one of them shall not fall on the ground without your Father. But the very hairs of your head are all numbered. Fear ye not therefore – ye are of more value than many sparrows.

Whosoever therefore shall confess me before men, him will I confess also before my Father which is in heaven. But whosoever shall deny me before men, him will I also deny before my Father which is in heaven.

Think not that I am come to send peace on earth: I came not to send peace, but a sword. For I am come to set a man at variance against his father, and the daughter against her mother, and the daughter-in-law against her mother-in-law. And a man's foes shall be they of his own household. He that loveth father or mother more than me is not worthy of me: and he that loveth son or daughter more than me is not worthy of me. And he that taketh not his cross, and followeth after me, is not worthy of me. He that findeth his life shall lose it; and he that loseth his life for my sake shall find it.

He that receiveth you receiveth me, and he that receiveth me receiveth him that sent me. He that receiveth a prophet in the name of a prophet shall receive a prophet's reward; and he that receiveth a righteous man in the name of a righteous man shall receive a righteous man's reward.

And whosoever shall give to drink unto one of

these little ones a cup of cold water only in the
name of a disciple, verily I say unto you, he shall in
no wise lose his reward.

They went out through the towns, and preached that men should repent. Healing everywhere, they anointed with oil many that were sick and cast out many unclean spirits.

Herod the tetrarch desires
to see Christ

Matthew 14:1–4, 13–14; Luke 9:7–11; Mark 6:17–18, 30–33

Now Herod the tetrarch heard of the fame of Jesus: and he was perplexed, because it was said by some that John was risen from the dead.

Herod himself had laid hold upon John, and bound him in prison for Herodias' sake, his brother Philip's wife: for John had said unto Herod, It is not lawful for thee to have thy brother's wife.

And Herod had married her: and later, at her daughter's request, he had sent an executioner and beheaded John in the prison. Herod said, John have I beheaded; so who is this of whom I hear such things? And he desired to see Jesus.

When the apostles were returned, and were gathered unto Jesus, they told all things, both what had come to pass and what they had taught.

Jesus said unto them,

Come ye yourselves apart into a desert place, and rest awhile.

He took his disciples, and went privately into a desert place belonging to the city called Bethsaida. He went up into a mountain, and there he sat with his disciples.

The people saw them departing, and many knew him, and ran afoot and outwent them, and came together unto him.

The feeding of the five thousand

John 6:5–13; Matthew 14:15–21; Mark 6:35–44; Luke 9:12–17

When Jesus saw a great company come unto him, he saith to Philip,

Whence shall we buy bread, that these may eat?

This he said to prove Philip, for he himself knew what he would do.

Jesus's disciples said, Shall we go and buy two hundred pennyworth of bread, and give them to eat?

Philip answered, Two hundred pennyworth of bread is not sufficient.

When the day began to wear away, then came the twelve and said, This is a desert place: send the multitude away, that they may go into the towns and villages round about, and lodge, and buy themselves victuals: for they have nothing to eat.

Jesus answered,

They need not depart; give ye them to eat. How many loaves have ye? Go and see.

Andrew, Simon Peter's brother, saith, A lad here hath five barley loaves, and two small fishes: but what are they among so many?

Jesus said,

Bring them hither to me. Make the men sit down by fifties in a company.

Now there was much green grass in the place. So the men sat down, in ranks, by hundreds and by fifties.

Jesus took the loaves, and when, looking up to heaven, he had given thanks, he blessed and brake, and distributed to the disciples, and the disciples to them that were set down; and likewise of the fishes, as much as they would.

They did all eat. And when they were filled, Jesus said unto his disciples,

Gather up the fragments that remain, that nothing be lost.

They filled twelve baskets. They that had eaten were about five thousand men, besides women and children.

Jesus walks on the water

Matthew 14:22–23; Mark 6:45–53; John 6:15–21

When Jesus perceived that they would take him by force, to make him a king, he constrained his disciples to get into a ship, and to go before him unto the other side, while he sent the multitude away.

He went up into a mountain apart, to pray: when the evening was come, he was there alone.

His disciples went over the sea toward Capernaum. The sea arose by reason of a great wind that blew. It was now dark, and the ship in the midst of the sea, tossed with the waves, and Jesus was on the land, alone.

He saw them toiling in rowing; and about the fourth watch of the night, they see Jesus walking on the sea, and drawing nigh unto the ship. They cried out for fear, saying, It is a spirit.

But straightway Jesus spoke,

Be of good cheer; it is I: be not afraid.

Peter answered, Lord, if it be thou, bid me come unto thee on the water.

Jesus said,

Come.

And Peter walked on the water, to go to Jesus. But he was afraid; and beginning to sink, he cried, Lord, save me.

Jesus stretched forth his hand, and caught him, and said,

O thou of little faith, wherefore didst thou doubt?

When they were come into the ship, the wind ceased. And when they had passed over, they came into the land of Gennesaret.

I am the bread of life

John 6:22–71

The day following, the people which stood on the other side of the sea from they did eat bread, when they saw that Jesus was not there, neither his disciples, took shipping and came to Capernaum, seeking him. And when they had found him, they said unto him, Master when camest thou hither?

Jesus answered,

Verily, verily, I say unto you, ye seek me, not because ye saw the miracles, but because ye did eat of the loaves and were filled. Labour not for the meat which perisheth, but for that meat which endureth unto everlasting life, which the Son of man shall give unto you: for him hath God the Father sealed.

Then asked they, What shall we do, that we might work the works of God?

Jesus answered,

This is the work of God, that ye believe on him whom he hath sent.

They said, What sign showest thou, then, that we may see and believe thee? Our fathers did eat manna in the desert; as it is written, He gave them bread from heaven.

Then said Jesus,

Verily, verily, I say unto you, Moses gave you not that bread from heaven; but my Father giveth you the true bread from heaven. For the bread of God is he which cometh down from heaven, and giveth life unto the world.

Then said they, Lord, evermore give us this bread.
And Jesus said,

I am the bread of life: he that cometh to me shall never hunger, and he that believeth on me shall never thirst. But I said unto you that ye also have seen me, and believe not.

All that the Father giveth me shall come to me, and him that cometh to me I will in no wise cast out.

For I came down from heaven, not to do mine own will, but the will of him that sent me. And this is the Father's will which hath sent me, that of all which he hath given me I should lose nothing, but should raise it up again at the last day. And this is the will of him that sent me, that everyone which seeth the Son, and believeth on him, may have everlasting life: and I will raise him up at the last day.

The Jews then murmured because he said, I am the bread which came down from heaven. And they said, Is not this Jesus, the son of Joseph, whose father and mother we know? How is it then that he saith, I came down from heaven?

Jesus answered,

Murmur not among yourselves. No man can come to me, except the Father which hath sent me draw him: and I will raise him up at the last day. It is written in the prophets, And they shall be all taught of God.

Every man therefore that hath heard, and hath learned of the Father, cometh unto me. Not that any man hath seen the Father, save he which is of God; he hath seen the Father.

Verily, verily, I say unto you, he that believeth on me hath everlasting life.

I am that bread of life.

Your fathers did eat manna in the wilderness, and are dead. This is the bread which cometh down from heaven, that a man may eat thereof, and not die. I am the living bread which came down from heaven: if any man eat of this bread, he shall live forever: and the bread that I will give is my flesh, which I will give for the life of the world.

The Jews therefore strove among themselves saying, How can this man give us his flesh to eat?

Then said Jesus,

Verily, verily, I say unto you, except ye eat the flesh of the Son of man, and drink his blood, ye have no life in you. Whoso eateth my flesh, and drinketh my blood, hath eternal life; and I will raise him up at the last day. For my flesh is meat indeed, and my blood is drink indeed. He that eateth my flesh, and drinketh my blood, dwelleth in me, and I in him. As the living Father hath sent me, and I live by the Father, so he that eateth me, even he shall live by

me. This is that bread which came down from
heaven: not as your fathers did eat manna, and are
dead: he that eateth of this bread shall live for ever.

These things said Jesus in the synagogue in Capernaum. Many
of his disciples said, This is a hard saying; who can hear it?

When Jesus knew in himself that his disciples murmured, he
said unto them,

Doth this offend you?

What and if ye shall see the Son of man ascend
up where he was before?

It is the Spirit that quickeneth; the flesh profiteth
nothing: the words that I speak unto you, they are
spirit, and they are life.

But there are some of you that believe not.

For Jesus knew from the beginning who they were that believed
not, and who should betray him. And he said,

Therefore said I unto you, that no man can come unto me, except it were given unto him of my Father.

From that time many of his disciples walked not with him. Then said Jesus unto the twelve,

Will ye also go away?

Simon Peter answered, Lord, to whom shall we go? thou hast the words of eternal life. And we are sure that thou art that Christ, the Son of the living God.

Jesus answered,

Have I not chosen you twelve, and one of you is a devil?

He spoke of Judas Iscariot; for he it was that should betray Jesus, being one of the twelve.

Jesus reproves the scribes and Pharisees

Mark 7:1–23; Matthew 15:1–20

Certain of the scribes saw some of Jesus's disciples eat bread with unwashed hands. They found fault: for the Pharisees, and all the Jews, except they wash their hands oft, eat not, holding the tradition of the elders. And many other traditions there be which they observe, such as the washing of cups and pots, brazen vessels and of tables.

The Pharisees and scribes asked Jesus, Why walk not thy disciples according to the tradition of the elders, but eat bread with unwashed hands? Why do thy disciples transgress?

But Jesus answered,

Why do ye also transgress the commandment of God by your tradition? Full well ye reject the commandment of God, that ye may keep your tradition. For God commanded, saying, Honour thy father and thy mother; and, Whoso curseth father or mother, let him die the death.

But ye say, Whosoever shall say to his father or his mother, It is Corban, that is to say, a gift, by whatsoever thou mightest be profited by me; and honour not his father or his mother: he shall be free. And ye suffer him no more to do aught for his father or his mother; making the word of God of none effect through your tradition, which ye have delivered; and many such like things do ye. Thus have ye made the commandment of God of none effect by your tradition.

Well hath Esaias prophesied of you hypocrites, as it is written, This people draweth nigh unto me with their mouth, this people honoureth me with their lips; but their heart is far from me. Howbeit in vain do they worship me, teaching for doctrines the commandments of men.

Ye hypocrites! for, laying aside the commandment of God, ye hold the tradition of men, as the washing of pots and cups: and many other suchlike things ye do.

And he called the multitude, and said unto them,

Hearken unto me every one of you. Hear, and understand. Not that which goeth into the mouth defileth a man. There is nothing from without a man that entering into him can defile him; but the things which come out of him, those are they that defile the man

If any man have ears to hear, let him hear.

His disciples, when he was entered into the house from the people, asked Jesus concerning the parable.

Jesus said,

Are ye also yet so without understanding? Do not ye yet perceive that whatsoever thing from without entereth into a man, entereth in at the mouth, goeth into the belly and is cast out into the draught, purging all meats? It entereth not into his heart; it cannot defile him.

But those things which proceed out of the mouth come forth from the heart, and they defile the man: for from within, out of the heart of men, proceed evil thoughts, adulteries, fornications, murders, thefts, covetousness, wickedness, false witness, deceit, lasciviousness, an evil eye, blasphemies, pride, foolishness: all these evil things come from within, and these are the things which defile the man; but to eat with unwashed hands defileth not a man.

Then his disciples said unto Jesus, Knowest thou that the Pharisees were offended, after they heard this saying?

But he answered,

Every plant which my heavenly Father hath not planted shall be rooted up. Let them alone: they be blind leaders of the blind. And if the blind lead the blind, both shall fall into the ditch.

Jesus performs two more miracles of healing

Matthew 15:21–28; Mark 7:24–36

From thence Jesus went into the borders of Tyre and Sidon.

And, behold, a Greek woman of Canaan came out of the same coasts, and cried unto him, saying, Have mercy on me, O Lord, thou Son of David: my daughter is grievously vexed with an unclean spirit.

Jesus answered her not a word. And his disciples came, saying, Send her away.

Jesus said,

I am not sent but unto the lost sheep of the house of Israel.

He entered into a house, and would have no man know it: but he could not be hid. For there came she whose young daughter had an unclean spirit, saying, Lord, help me.

But Jesus said unto her,

Let the children first be filled: for it is not meet to take the children's bread, and to cast it unto the dogs.

She said, Yes, Lord: yet the dogs under the table eat of the children's crumbs which fall from their master's table.

Jesus answered,

O woman, great is thy faith: be it unto thee even as thou wilt. For this saying go thy way; the devil is gone out of thy daughter.

Her daughter was made whole from that very hour.

Departing from the coasts of Tyre and Sidon, Jesus came unto the sea of Galilee, through the midst of the coasts of Decapolis.

They brought unto him one that was deaf, and had an impediment in his speech. Jesus took him aside, and put his fingers into his ears and touched his tongue; and looking up to heaven he sighed, and said,

Be opened.

Straightway his ears were opened, and the string of his tongue was loosed and he spoke clearly.

Jesus charged them that they should tell no man: but the more he charged them not to, the more they published it abroad.

The feeding of the four thousand, and what followed

Mark 8:1–26; Matthew 15:32–39; 16:1–12; John 6:1–12

In those days, the multitude being great and having nothing to eat, Jesus called his disciples, and said,

I have compassion on the multitude, because they have now been with me three days, and have nothing to eat: and if I send them away fasting to their own houses, they will faint by the way.

For divers of them came from far.

His disciples were at a loss, and asked, From whence can we satisfy these men with bread here in the wilderness?

Jesus said,

I will not send them away fasting, lest they faint in the way. How many loaves have ye?

They said, Seven, and a few little fishes.

He commanded the people to sit on the ground: and he took the seven loaves, and gave thanks, and brake, and gave to his disciples to set before the people. The few small fishes he blessed and commanded to be set also before them.

So they did all eat, and were filled, and of the broken meat that was left, they took up seven baskets full. And they that had eaten were about four thousand, besides women and children.

Having sent the people away, Jesus entered into a ship with his disciples and came into the coasts of Magdala. The Pharisees with the Sadducees came forth to question him, seeking of him a sign from heaven, tempting him.

He sighed deeply in his spirit, and said,

Why doth this generation seek after a sign? Verily I say unto you, there shall no sign be given unto this generation.

When it is evening, ye say, It will be fair weather: for the sky is red. And in the morning, It will be foul weather today: for the sky is red and lowering. O ye hypocrites, ye can discern the face of the sky; but can ye not discern the signs of the times? A wicked and adulterous generation seeketh after a sign; and there shall no sign be given unto it, but the sign of the prophet Jonas.

Entering into the ship again, Jesus departed to the other side. Now the disciples had forgotten to take bread; neither had they in the ship with them more than one loaf.

Then Jesus charged them,

Take heed and beware of the leaven of the Pharisees and of the Sadducees, and of the leaven of Herod.

They reasoned among themselves, saying, It is because we have taken no heed.

Which when Jesus perceived, he said unto them,

O ye of little faith, why reason ye among yourselves,

because ye have brought no bread? Perceive ye not yet, neither understand? Have ye your heart yet hardened? Having eyes, see ye not? and having ears, hear ye not? and do ye not remember?

Do ye not understand, neither remember the five loaves of the five thousand, and how many baskets ye took up? Neither the seven loaves of the four thousand, and how many baskets ye took up?

When I brake the five loaves among the five thousand, how many baskets full of fragments took ye up?

They answer, Twelve.

And when the seven among four thousand, how many baskets full of fragments took ye up?

They said, Seven.
And Jesus said,

How is it that ye do not understand that I spake it not to you concerning bread, that ye should beware of the leaven of the Pharisees and of the Sadducees?

Then understood they how he bade them not beware of the leaven of bread, but of the doctrine of the Pharisees and the Sadducees.

Ater this, Jesus came to Bethsaida; and they brought a blind man to him. He took the man by the hand, and led him out of the town, and having put his hands upon his eyes, asked him if he could see anything. The man looked up, and said, I see men as trees, walking. Jesus again put his hands upon his eyes, and made him look up, and his sight was fully restored, and he saw every man clearly.

Jesus sent him away, saying,

Neither go into the town, nor tell it to any in the town.

Christ discloses his Sonship

Matthew 16:13–28; Mark 8:27–38; 9:1; Luke 9:18–27

Jesus and his disciples came into the towns of Cesarea Philippi. And by the way he asked them.

Whom do men say that I, the Son of man, am? Whom say the people that I am?

They answering said, John the Baptist; but some say, Elias; and others, Jeremias; and others say that one of the old prophets is risen again.

Jesus said,

But whom say ye that I am?

Simon Peter answering said, Thou art the Christ, the Son of the living God.

Jesus said to Peter,

Blessed art thou, Simon Bar-jona: for flesh and

blood hath not revealed it unto thee, but my Father which is in heaven.

And I say unto thee that thou art Peter, and upon this rock I will build my church; and the gates of hell shall not prevail against it.

And I will give unto thee the keys of the kingdom of heaven: and whatsoever thou shalt bind on earth shall be bound in heaven; and whatsoever thou shalt loose on earth shall be loosed in heaven.

And he straitly charged them that they should tell no man of him: that he was Jesus the Christ.

From that time forth began Jesus to show to his disciples how he, the Son of man, must go unto Jerusalem and be killed, saying,

The Son of man must suffer many things, and be rejected of the elders and chief priests and scribes, and be slain, and be raised the third day.

He spake that saying openly.

Then Peter began to rebuke him, saying, Be it far from thee, Lord: this shall not be unto thee.

When Jesus had turned and looked on his disciples, he rebuked Peter, saying,

Get thee behind me, Satan: thou are an offence unto me: for thou savourest not the things that be of God, but the things that be of men.

When he had called the people unto him, with his disciples also, he said unto them,

If any man will come after me, let him deny himself and take up his cross daily and follow me.

For whosoever will save his life shall lose it: but whosoever will lose his life for my sake and the gospel's, the same shall save it. For what shall it profit a man, what is a man advantaged, if he gain the whole world and lose his own soul? or be cast

away? Or what shall a man give in exchange for his soul? For the Son of man shall come in the glory of his Father with his angels; and then he shall reward every man according to his works.

Whosoever therefore shall be ashamed of me and of my words, in this adulterous and sinful generation, of him also shall the Son of man be ashamed, when he shall come in his own glory: and cometh in the glory of his Father with his holy angels.

But I tell you of a truth, there be some standing here which shall not taste of death till they have seen the kingdom of God come with power, the Son of man coming in his kingdom.

Jesus transfigured

Luke 9:28–42; Matthew 17:1–21; Mark 9:2–29

It came to pass, about eight days after these sayings, that Jesus took Peter, John and James and went up into a high mountain apart to pray: and Jesus was transfigured before them.

As he prayed, the fashion of his countenance was altered: his face did shine as the sun, and his raiment was white as the light, and glistering, shining as snow, exceeding white, whiter than any fuller on earth can whiten.

And, behold, two men, Moses and Elias, appeared in glory, talking with Jesus of his decease, which he should accomplish at Jerusalem.

Peter and they that were with Jesus saw his glory, and the two men with Jesus.

There came a bright cloud that overshadowed them: and a voice out of the cloud, saying, This is my beloved Son, in whom I am well pleased; hear ye him.

The disciples fell on their faces and were sore afraid.

Jesus came and touched them, and said,

Arise, and be not afraid.

And when they had lifted up their eyes, they saw no man any more, save Jesus only.

And he charged them,

Tell the vision to no man, until the Son of man be risen again from the dead.

Questioning with one another what the rising from the dead should mean, his disciples asked Jesus, Why say the scribes that Elias must first come?

Jesus told them,

Elias verily cometh first, and restoreth all things; and how it is written of the Son of man, that he must suffer many things and be set at nought.

But I say unto you that Elias is indeed come already, and they knew him not; and they have done unto him whatsoever they listed, as it is written of him. Likewise shall also the Son of man suffer of them.

The disciples understood that he spoke of John the Baptist. They kept it close, and told no man in those days any of the things which they had seen.

When Jesus saw a multitude about his disciples and the scribes questioning with them, he asked the scribes,

What question ye with them?

One of the multitude answered, Master, I have brought unto thee my son: Lord, have mercy, for he is lunatic and sore vexed: oft-times he falleth into the fire, and oft into the water. A spirit teareth him that he foameth again, and gnasheth his teeth, and pineth away. I brought him to thy disciples, and they could not cure him. He is mine only child.

Then Jesus said,

O faithless and perverse generation, how long shall I be with you? How long shall I suffer you?
    Bring thy son hither to me.

They brought him: and as he was yet coming, the spirit tore him, and he fell and wallowed, foaming.

Jesus asked his father,

How long is it ago since this came unto him?

He said, Of a child. Have compassion on us.

Jesus said,

If thou canst believe, all things are possible to him that believeth.

Straightway the father said with tears, Lord, I believe; help thou my unbelief.

Jesus rebuked the foul spirit, saying,

Thou dumb and deaf spirit, I charge thee, come out of him and enter no more into him.

The child was cured from that very hour.

When Jesus was come into the house, his disciples asked him privately, Why could not we cast him out?

Jesus answered.

Because of your unbelief: for verily I say unto you, if ye have faith as a grain of mustard seed, ye shall say unto this mountain, Remove hence; and it shall remove; and nothing shall be impossible unto you. Howbeit, this kind goeth not out but by prayer and fasting.

Jesus foretells his death and preaches concerning other matters

Mark 9:30–37; Luke 9:44–48; Matthew 17:22–27

Jesus departed thence, and passed through Galilee. While in Galilee, Jesus said unto his disciples,

Let these sayings sink down into your ears: for the Son of man shall be betrayed, and delivered into the hands of men: and they shall kill him; and the third day after that he is killed, he shall be raised again.

But they understood not.

There arose a reasoning among the disciples: for by the way to Capernaum they had disputed amongst themselves which of them should be the greatest.

In the house, Jesus asked,

What was it that ye disputed among yourselves by the way?

But they held their peace: and Jesus, perceiving the thought of their heart, said,

If any man desire to be first, the same shall be last of all, and servant of all.

He took a child in his arms, and said,

Whosoever shall receive this child in my name, receiveth me; whosoever shall receive one of such children in my name, receiveth me; and whosoever shall receive me, receiveth me not, but him that sent me; for he that is least among you all, the same shall be great.

When they were in Capernaum, they that received tribute money came to Peter, and said, Doth not your master pay tribute?

Peter said, Yes.

And when he was come into the house, Jesus prevented him, saying,

What thinkest thou, Simon? Of whom do the kings of the earth take custom or tribute? of their own children, or of strangers?

Peter saith, Of strangers.
Jesus answered,

Then are the children free.

Notwithstanding, lest we should offend them, go thou to the sea, and cast a hook, and take up the fish that first cometh up; and when thou hast opened his mouth, thou shalt find a piece of money: that take, and give unto them for me and thee.

John is answered

Mark 9:38–50; Luke 9:49–50

John said, Master, we saw one casting out devils in thy name: and we forbade him, because he followeth not us.

But Jesus said,

Forbid him not: for there is no man which shall do a miracle in my name that can lightly speak evil of me. For he that is not against us is for us, is on our part.

For whosoever shall give you a cup of water to drink in my name, because ye belong to Christ, verily I say unto you, he shall not lose his reward.

And whosoever shall offend one of these little ones that believe in me, it is better for him that a millstone were hanged about his neck, and he were cast into the sea.

And if thy hand offend thee, cut it off: it is better for thee to enter into life maimed, than having two hands to go into hell, into the fire that never shall be quenched: where their worm dieth not, and the fire is not quenched.

And if thy foot offend thee, cut it off: it is better for thee to enter halt into life, than having two feet to be cast into hell, into the fire that never shall be quenched: where their worm dieth not, and the fire is not quenched.

And if thine eye offend thee, pluck it out: it is better for thee to enter into the kingdom of God with one eye, than having two eyes to be cast into hell fire: where their worm dieth not, and the fire is not quenched.

For everyone shall be salted with fire, and every sacrifice shall be salted with salt. Salt is good: but if the salt have lost his saltness, wherewith will ye season it? Have salt in yourselves, and have peace one with another.

Jesus teaches his disciples humility and forgivenesss

Matthew 18:1–35

At the same time came the disciples unto Jesus, saying, Who is the greatest in the kingdom of heaven?

And Jesus called a little child unto him, set him in the midst of them, and said,

Verily I say unto you, except ye be converted, and become as little children, ye shall not enter into the kingdom of heaven.

Whosoever therefore shall humble himself as this little child, the same is greatest in the kingdom of heaven. And whoso shall receive one such little child in my name receiveth me.

But whoso shall offend one of these little ones which believe in me, it were better for him that a

millstone were hanged about his neck, and that he were drowned in the depth of the sea.

Woe unto the world because of offences! For it must needs be that offences come; but woe to that man by whom the offence cometh!

Wherefore, if thy hand or thy foot offend thee, cut them off, and cast them from thee: it is better for thee to enter into life halt or maimed, rather than having two hands or two feet to be cast into everlasting fire.

And if thine eye offend thee, pluck it out, and cast it from thee: it is better for thee to enter into life with one eye, rather than having two eyes to be cast into hell fire.

Take heed that ye despise not one of these little ones; for I say unto you that in heaven their angels do always behold the face of my Father which is in heaven. For the Son of man is come to save that which was lost.

How think ye? if a man have a hundred sheep, and one of them be gone astray, doth he not leave the ninety and nine, and go into the mountains, and seek that which is gone astray? And if so be that he find it, verily I say unto you, he rejoiceth more of that sheep, than of the ninety and nine which went not astray. Even so, it is not the will of your Father which is in heaven that one of these little ones should perish.

Moreover, if thy brother shall trespass against thee, go and tell him his fault between thee and him alone: if he shall hear thee, thou hast gained thy brother. But if he will not hear thee, then take with thee one or two more, that in the mouth of two or three witnesses every word may be established. And *if he shall neglect to hear them, tell it unto the church: but if he neglect to hear the church, let him be unto thee as a heathen man and a publican.*

Verily 1 say unto you, whatsoever ye shall bind on earth shall be bound in heaven: and whatsoever ye shall loose on earth shall be loosed in heaven.

Again, I say unto you that if two of you shall agree on earth as touching anything that they shall ask, it shall be done for them of my Father which is in heaven. For where two or three are gathered together in my name, there am I in the midst of them.

Then Peter said, Lord, how oft shall my brother sin against me, and I forgive him? till seven times?

Jesus said,

I say not unto thee, until seven times: but, until seventy times seven.

Therefore is the kingdom of heaven likened unto a certain king, which would take account of his servants. And when he had begun to reckon, one was brought unto him which owed him ten thousand talents. But forasmuch as he had not to pay, his lord commanded him to be sold, and his wife and children and all that he had, and payment to be made. The servant therefore fell down and worshipped him, saying, Lord, have patience with me, and I will pay thee all. Then the lord of that servant was moved with compassion and loosed him, and forgave him the debt.

But the same servant went out, and found one of his fellow servants, which owed him a hundred pence: and he laid hands on him, and took him by the throat, saying, Pay me that thou owest. And his fellow servant fell down at his feet, and besought him, saying, Have patience with me, and I will pay thee all. And he would not but went and cast him into prison, till he should pay the debt.

So when his fellow servants saw what was done, they were very sorry, and came and told unto their lord all that was done. Then his lord, after that he had called him, said unto him, O thou wicked servant, I forgave thee all that debt, because thou desiredst me; shouldest not thou also have had compassion on thy fellow servant, even as I had pity on thee?

And his lord was wroth, and delivered him to the tormentors, till he should pay all that was due unto him. So likewise shall my heavenly Father do also unto you, if ye from your hearts forgive not every one his brother their trespasses.

At the feast of the Tabernacles

John 7:1–46, 53; 8:1

After these things, Jesus walked in Galilee: for he would not walk in Jewry, because the Jews sought to kill him.

Now the Jews feast of the Tabernacles was at hand. Jesus's brethren therefore said unto him, Go into Judea, that thy disciples there may see the works that thou doest. For no man that doeth anything in secret can hope to be known for it openly. If thou do these things, show thyself to the world.

Then Jesus said,

My time is not yet come: but your time is always ready. The world cannot hate you; but me it hateth, because I testify of it that the works thereof are evil. Go ye up unto this feast: for my time is not yet full come.

Jesus abode still in Galilee.

But when his brethren were gone up, then went he also up unto the feast, not openly, but as it were in secret.

There was much murmuring among the people concerning him: for some said, He is a good man; others said, Nay; but he deceiveth the people.

Howbeit no man spoke openly of him for fear of the Jews. The Jews sought him at the feast.

Now about the midst of the feast Jesus went up into the temple and taught. The Jews marvelled, saying, How knoweth this man letters, having never learned?

Jesus answered,

My doctrine is not mine, but his that sent me. If any man will do his will, he shall know of the doctrine, whether it be of God or whether I speak of myself. He that speaketh of himself seeketh his own glory: but he that seeketh his glory that sent him, the same is true, and no unrighteousness is in him.

Did not Moses give you the law, and yet none of you keepeth the law? Why go ye about to kill me?

The people answered, Who goeth about to kill thee? Thou hast a devil.

Jesus answered,

I have done one work, and ye all marvel.

Moses therefore gave unto you circumcision (not because it is of Moses but of the fathers); and ye on the sabbath day circumcise a man. If a man on the sabbath day receive circumcision, that the law of Moses should not be broken, why are ye angry at me, because I have made a man every whit whole on the sabbath day?

Judge not according to the appearance, but judge righteous judgment.

Then said some of them of Jerusalem, Is not this he whom they seek to kill? But, lo, he speaketh boldly, and they say nothing unto him. Do the rulers know indeed that this is the very Christ? Howbeit we know this man whence he is, but when

Christ cometh, no man knoweth whence he is.

Then cried Jesus in the temple as he taught, saying,

Ye both know me, and ye know whence I am: and I am not come of myself, but he that sent me is true, whom ye know not. But I know him; for I am from him, and he hath sent me.

Then they sought to take him: but his hour was not yet come. Many believed on Jesus, and said, When Christ cometh, will he do more miracles than those which this man hath done?

The Pharisees and chief priests heard that the people murmured such things concerning Jesus, and sent officers to take him.

Then said Jesus,

Yet a little while am I with you, and then I go unto him that sent me. Ye shall seek me, and shall not find me: and where I am, thither ye cannot come.

Then said the Jews among themselves, What manner of saying

is this that he said, Ye shall seek me, and shall not find me: and where I am, thither ye cannot come?

In the last day, that great day of the feast, Jesus stood and cried,

If any man thirst, let him come unto me and drink. He that believeth on me, as the scripture hath said, out of his belly shall flow rivers of living water.

Many of the people, when they heard this saying, said, Of a truth this is the Prophet. Others said, This is the Christ. But some said, Shall Christ come out of Galilee?

So there was a division among the people because of him. And some of them would have taken him; but no man laid hands upon him.

Then came the officers to the chief priests and Pharisees. They said, Why have ye not brought him?

The officers answered, Never man spake like this man.

And every man went unto his own home. Jesus went unto the Mount of Olives.

Jesus shames a woman's accusers
and confutes the Jews

John 8:2–59

Early in the morning Jesus came again into the temple. The people came; and he sat down, and taught them.

The scribes and Pharisees brought a woman taken in adultery. They say unto Jesus, Master, Moses in the law commanded us that such should be stoned: but what sayest thou?

This they said, tempting him, that they might be able to accuse him.

But Jesus stooped, and with his finger wrote on the ground, as though he heard them not. So when they continued asking him, he lifted up himself, and said unto them,

He that is without sin among you, let him first cast a stone at her.

Again Jesus stooped, and wrote on the ground. And they, being convicted by their own conscience, went out one by one, beginning at the eldest: Jesus was left alone with the woman.

When he had lifted up himself, and saw none but the woman, he said,

Woman, where are those thine accusers? Hath no man condemned thee?

She said, No man, Lord.
And Jesus said unto her,

Neither do I condemn thee: go, and sin no more.

Jesus spoke again unto the people, saying,

I am the light of the world: he that followeth me shall not walk in darkness, but shall have the light of life.

The Pharisees therefore said, Thou bearest record of thyself; thy record is not true.
Jesus answered,

Though I bear record of myself, yet my record is

true: for I know whence I came, and whither I go;
but ye cannot tell whence I come, and whither I go.

Ye judge after the flesh; I judge no man. And yet
if I judge, my judgment is true: for I am not alone,
but I and the Father that sent me.

It is also written in your law that the testimony of
two men is true. I am one that bear witness of
myself, and the Father that sent me beareth witness
of me.

Then said they. Where is thy father?
Jesus answered,

Ye neither know me, nor my Father: if ye had
known me, ye should have known my Father also.

These words spake Jesus in the treasury, as he taught in the
temple: and no man laid hands on him; for his hour was not yet
come.

Then said Jesus again,

I go my way, and ye shall seek me, and shall die in your sins; whither I go, ye cannot come.

Then said the Jews, Will he kill himself? because he saith, Whither I go, ye cannot come.
And he said.

Ye are from beneath; I am from above: ye are of this world; I am not of this world. I said therefore unto you that ye shall die in your sins: for if ye believe not that I am he, ye shall die in your sins.

Then said they, Who art thou?
And Jesus answered,

Even the same that I said unto you from the beginning.

  I have many things to say and to judge of you:

but he that sent me is true; and I speak to the world those things which I have heard of him.

They understood not that he spoke to them of the Father. Then said Jesus,

When ye have lifted up the Son of man, then shall ye know that I am he, and that I do nothing of myself; but as my Father hath taught me, I speak these things. And he that sent me is with me: the Father hath not left me alone; for I do always those things that please him.

As he spake these words, many believed. Then said Jesus to those Jews which believed on him,

If ye continue in my word, then are ye my disciples indeed; and ye shall know the truth, and the truth shall make you free.

They answered, We be Abraham's seed, and were never in bondage to any man: how sayest thou, Ye shall be made free?

Jesus answered,

Verily, verily, I say unto you, whosoever committeth sin is the servant of sin. And the servant abideth not in the house for ever: but the Son abideth ever. If the Son therefore shall make you free, ye shall be free indeed.

I know that ye are Abraham's seed; but ye seek to kill me, because my word hath no place in you. I speak that which I have seen with my Father: and ye do that which ye have seen with your father.

They answered, Abraham is our father.
Jesus replied,

If ye were Abraham's children, ye would do the works of Abraham. But now ye seek to kill me, a man that hath told you the truth, which I have heard of God: this did not Abraham. Ye do the deeds of your father.

Then they said, We be not born of fornication: we have one Father, even God.

Jesus answered,

If God were your Father, ye would love me: for I proceeded forth and came from God; neither came I of myself, but he sent me.

Why do ye not understand my speech? even because ye cannot hear my word. Ye are of your father the devil, and the lusts of your father ye will do: he was a murderer from the beginning, and abode not in the truth, because there is no truth in him. When he speaketh a lie, he speaketh of his own: for he is a liar, and the father of it.

And because I tell you the truth, ye believe me not. Which of you convinceth me of sin? And if I say the truth, why do ye not believe me? He that is of God heareth God's words: ye therefore hear them not, because ye are not of God.

Then answered the Jews, Say we not well that thou art a Samaritan, and hast a devil?

Jesus answered,

I have not a devil; but I honour my Father, and ye do dishonour me. And I seek not mine own glory: there is one that seeketh and judgeth.

Verily, verily, I say unto you, if a man keep my saying, he shall never see death.

Then said the Jews, Now we know that thou hast a devil. Abraham is dead, and the prophets, and thou sayest, If a man keep my saying, he shall never taste of death. Art thou greater than our father Abraham, which is dead? And the prophets are dead. Who makest thou thyself?

Jesus answered,

If I honour myself, my honour is nothing: it is my Father that honoureth me; of whom ye say that he is your God: yet ye have not known him: but I know him: and if I should say, I know him not, I shall be a liar like unto you; but I know him, and keep his saying. Your father Abraham rejoiced to see my day; and he saw it, and was glad.

Then said the Jews, Thou art not yet fifty years old, and hast thou seen Abraham?

Jesus answered,

Verily, verily I say unto you, before Abraham was, I am.

They took up stones to cast at him; but Jesus hid himself, and went out of the temple, going through the midst of them, and so passed by.

Jesus heals a man born blind and describes himself as the good shepherd

John 9:1–41; 10:1–18, 22–40

As Jesus passed by, he saw a man which was blind from his birth. His disciples asked, Master, who did sin, this man, or his parents, that he was born blind?

Jesus answered,

Neither hath this man sinned, nor his parents: but that the works of God should be made manifest in him.

I must work the works of him that sent me, while it is day; the night cometh, when no man can work. As long as I am in the world, I am the light of the world.

When he had thus spoken, he anointed the eyes of the blind man with clay, and said unto him,

Go, wash in the pool of Siloam.

He went, and washed, and came seeing.

The neighbours said, Is not this he that sat and begged?

He answered, I am he.

Therefore, said they, how were thine eyes opened?

He said, A man called Jesus made clay, and anointed mine, eyes, and said unto me, Go to the pool of Siloam, and wash: and I went and washed, and I received sight.

It was the sabbath day when Jesus opened his eyes. Therefore said some of the Pharisees, This man is not of God, because he keepeth not the sabbath day. Others said, How can a man that is a sinner do such miracles? And there was a division among them.

The Jews called the parents, and asked them, Is this your son, who was born blind? How then doth he now see?

His parents answered, We know that this is our son, and that he was born blind: but by what means he now seeth, we know not; he is of age; ask him.

His parents feared the Jews: for the Jews had agreed already that if any man did confess that Jesus was Christ, he should be put out of the synagogue.

Again the Jews called the man that was blind, and said unto him, Give God the praise: we know that this man Jesus is a sinner: we know not from whence he is.

The man answered, Why! herein is a marvellous thing, that ye know not from whence he is, and yet he hath opened mine eyes. Now we know that God heareth not sinners: but if any man be a worshipper of God, and doeth his will, him he heareth. If this man were not of God, he could do nothing.

They answered, Thou wast altogether born in sin, and dost thou teach us? And they cast him out.

Jesus found him and said to him,

Dost thou believe on the Son of God?

He answered, Who is he, Lord, that I might believe on him? Jesus said,

Thou hast both seen him, and it is he that talketh with thee.

And he said, Lord, I believe.

Jesus said,

For judgment I am come into this world, that they which see not might see; and that they which see might be made blind.

Some of the Pharisees heard these words, and said, Are we blind also?

Jesus answered,

If ye were blind, ye should have no sin: but now ye say, We see; therefore your sin remaineth.

This parable spoke Jesus unto them,

Verily, verily, I say unto you, he that entereth not by the door into the sheepfold but climbeth up some other way, the same is a thief and a robber. But he that entereth in by the door is the shepherd of the sheep. To him the porter openeth; and the sheep hear his voice: and he calleth his own sheep by name, and leadeth them out.

And when he putteth forth his own sheep, he goeth before them, and the sheep follow him: for they know his voice. And a stranger will they not follow, but will flee from him: for they know not the voice of strangers.

But they understood not.
Then said Jesus,

Verily, verily, I say unto you, I am the door of the sheep. All that ever came before me are thieves and robbers: but the sheep did not hear them.

I am the door: by me if any man enter in, he shall be saved, and shall go in and out, and find pasture.

The thief cometh not but for to steal, and to kill, and to destroy: I am come that they might have life, and that they might have it more abundantly.

I am the good shepherd: the good shepherd giveth his life for the sheep. But he that is a hireling, and not the shepherd, whose own the sheep are not, seeth the wolf coming, and leaveth the sheep, and fleeth: and the wolf catcheth them and scattereth the sheep. The hireling fleeth, because he is a hireling, and careth not for the sheep.

I am the good shepherd, and know my sheep, and am known of mine. As the Father knoweth me, even so know I the Father and I lay down my life for the sheep.

And other sheep I have which are not of this fold: them also I must bring, and they shall hear my voice; and there shall be one fold, and one shepherd.

Therefore doth my Father love me, because I lay

down my life, that I might take it again. No man
taketh it from me, but I lay it down of myself. I have
power to lay it down, and I have power to take it
again. This commandment have I received of my
Father.

At Jerusalem it was the feast of the dedication. It was winter.
Jesus walked in the temple in Solomon's porch.

Then came the Jews round about him, and said, How long
dost thou make us to doubt? If thou be the Christ, tell us plainly.

Jesus answered,

I told you, and ye believed not: the works that I do
in my Father's name, they bear witness of me. But
ye believe not, because ye are not of my sheep, as I
said unto you. My sheep hear my voice, and I know
them, and they follow me: and I give unto them
eternal life; and they shall never perish, neither
shall any man pluck them out of my hand.

My Father, which gave them me, is greater than all; and no man is able to pluck them out of my Father's hand.

I and my Father are one.

The Jews took up stones again to stone him.
Jesus asked them,

Many good works have I showed you from my Father; for which of those works do ye stone me?

The Jews answered, For a good work we stone thee not; but for blasphemy; and because that thou makest thyself God.
Jesus answered,

Is it not written in your law, I said, Ye are gods?

If he called them gods, unto whom the word of God came, and the scripture cannot be broken; say ye of him, whom the Father hath sanctified and sent into the world, Thou blasphemest; because I said, I am the Son of God?

If I do not the works of my Father, believe me not. But if I do, though ye believe not me, believe the works; that ye may know, and believe, that the Father is in me, and I in him.

Therefore they sought again to take him: but he escaped out of their hand, and went away again beyond Jordan into the place where John at first baptized; and there he abode.

Jesus sends out seventy disciples

Luke 9:51–62; 10:1–24

When the time was come that Jesus should be received up, he steadfastly set his face to go to Jerusalem, and sent messengers before: they entered into a village of the Samaritans.

When the villagers would not receive him, James and John said, Lord wilt thou that we command fire to come down and consume them, as Elias did?

But he rebuked them, saying,

Ye know not what manner of spirit ye are of. For the Son of man is not come to destroy men's lives, but to save them.

They went to another village. In the way, a certain man said unto Jesus, Lord, I will follow thee whithersoever thou goest.

Jesus said unto him,

Foxes have holes, and birds of the air have nests; but the Son of man hath not where to lay his head.

And he said unto another,

Follow me.

But he said, Lord, suffer me first to go and bury my father. Jesus said to him,

Let the dead bury their dead: but go thou and preach the kingdom of God.

Another said, Lord, I will follow thee; but let me first go bid them farewell which are at home at my house.
Jesus said unto him,

No man, having put his hand to the plough, and looking back, is fit for the kingdom of God.

After these things the Lord appointed another seventy, and sent them two and two before his face into every city and place whither he himself would come. Therefore said he unto them,

The harvest truly is great, but the labourers are

few: pray ye therefore the Lord of the harvest that he send forth labourers into his harvest.

Go your ways: behold, I send you forth as lambs among wolves. Carry neither purse, nor scrip, nor shoes: and salute no man by the way.

And into whatsoever house ye enter, first say, Peace be to this house. And if the son of peace be there, your peace shall rest upon it: if not, it shall turn to you again.

And in the same house remain, eating and drinking such things as they give: for the labourer is worthy of his hire. Go not from house to house.

And into whatsoever city ye enter, and they receive you, eat such things as are set before you: and heal the sick that are therein, and say unto them, The kingdom of God is come nigh unto you.

But into whatsoever city ye enter, and they receive you not, go your ways out into the streets of the same, and say, Even the very dust of your city, which cleaveth on us, we do wipe off against you; notwithstanding, be ye sure of this, that the kingdom of God is come nigh unto you.

But I say unto you, that it shall be more tolerable in that day for Sodom, than for that city.

Woe unto thee, Chorazin! woe unto thee Bethsaida! for if the mighty works had been done in Tyre and Sidon, which have been done in you, they had a great while ago repented, sitting in sackcloth and ashes. But it shall be more tolerable for Tyre and Sidon at the judgment, than for you.

And thou, Capernaum, which art exalted to heaven, shalt be thrust down to hell.

He that heareth you heareth me; and he that despiseth you despiseth me; and he that despiseth me despiseth him that sent me.

The seventy returned with joy, saying, Lord, even the devils are subject unto us through thy name.

Jesus said unto them,

I beheld Satan as lightning fall from heaven. Behold, I give unto you power to tread on serpents and scorpions, and over all the power of the enemy; and nothing shall by any means hurt you. Notwithstanding, in this rejoice not that the spirits are subject unto you; but rather rejoice because your names are written in heaven.

In that hour Jesus rejoiced in spirit, and said,

I thank thee, O Father, Lord of heaven and earth,

that thou hast hid these things from the wise and prudent, and has revealed them unto babes; even so, Father, for so it seemed good in thy sight.

All things are delivered to me of my Father: and no man knoweth who the Son is, but the Father; and who the Father is, but the Son, and he to whom the Son will reveal him.

He turned to his disciples, and said privately,

Blessed are the eyes which see the things that ye see: for I tell you that many prophets and kings have desired to see those things which ye see, and have not seen them; and to hear those things which ye hear, and have not heard them.

The good Samaritan

Luke 10:25–37

A certain lawyer stood up, and tempted Jesus, saying, Master, what shall I do to inherit eternal life?

Jesus said,

What is written in the law? How readest thou?

He answering said, Thou shalt love the Lord thy God with all thy heart, and with all thy soul, and with all thy strength, and with all thy mind; and thy neighbour as thyself.

Jesus said unto him,

Thou hast answered right: this do, and thou shalt live.

But he, willing to justify himself, said, And who is my neighbour?

Jesus answering said,

A certain man went down from Jerusalem to

Jericho, and fell among thieves, which stripped him of his raiment, and wounded him, and departed, leaving him half dead.

And by chance there came down a certain priest that way: and when he saw him, he passed by on the other side.

And likewise a Levite, when he was at the place, came and looked on him, and passed by on the other side.

But a certain Samaritan, as he journeyed, came where he was: and when he saw him, he had compassion on him, and went to him, and bound up his wounds, pouring in oil and wine, and set him on his own beast, and brought him to an inn, and took care of him. And on the morrow when he departed, he took out two pence, and gave them to *the host, and said unto him, Take care of him: and whatsoever thou spendest more, when I come again, I will repay thee.*

Which now of these three, thinkest thou, was neighbour unto him that fell among the thieves?

He said, He that showed mercy on him.
Then said Jesus unto him,

Go, and do thou likewise.

Parables and precepts

Luke 11:1–13, 27–54

Jesus was praying in a certain place, and when he ceased one of his disciples said unto him, Lord, teach us to pray, as John also taught his disciples.

Jesus said unto them,

When ye pray, say, Our Father which art in heaven, hallowed be thy name. Thy kingdom come. Thy will be done, as in heaven, so in earth.

Give us day by day our daily bread.

And forgive us our sins; for we also forgive everyone that is indebted to us.

And lead us not into temptation; but deliver us from evil.

And he said unto them,

Which of you shall have a friend, and shall go unto him at midnight, and say unto him, Friend, lend me three loaves, for a friend of mine in his journey is come to me, and I have nothing to set before him? And he from within shall answer and say, Trouble me not: the door is now shut, and my children are with me in bed; I cannot rise and give thee.

I say unto you, Though he will not rise and give him, because he is his friend, yet because of his importunity he will rise and give him as many as he needeth.

And I say unto you, Ask, and it shall be given you; seek, and ye shall find; knock, and it shall be opened unto you. For everyone that asketh receiveth; and he that seeketh findeth; and to him that knocketh it shall be opened.

If a son shall ask bread of any of you that is a father, will he give him a stone? or if he ask a fish, will he for a fish give him a serpent? Or if he shall ask an egg, will he offer him a scorpion?

If ye then, being evil, know how to give good gifts unto your children; how much more shall your heavenly Father give the Holy Spirit to them that ask him?

And it came to pass, while he was speaking, a certain woman of the company lifted up her voice, and said, Blessed is the womb that bare thee, and the paps which thou hast sucked.

But Jesus said,

Yea, rather, blessed are they that hear the word of God, and keep it.

When the people were gathered thick together, he began to say,

This is an evil generation: they seek a sign; and there shall no sign be given it, but the sign of Jonas the prophet. For as Jonas was a sign unto the Ninevites, so shall also the Son of man be to this generation.

The queen of the south shall rise up in the judgment with the men of this generation, and condemn them: for she came from the utmost parts of the earth to hear the wisdom of Solomon; and, behold, a greater than Solomon is here.

The men of Nineveh shall rise up in the judgment with this generation, and shall condemn it: for they repented at the preaching of Jonas; and, behold, a greater than Jonas is here.

No man, when he hath lighted a candle, putteth it in a secret place, neither under a bushel, but on a candlestick, that they which come in may see the light. The light of the body is the eye: therefore when thine eye is single, thy whole body also is full of light; but when thine eye is evil, thy body also is full of darkness. Take heed therefore that the light which is in thee be not darkness. If thy whole body therefore be full of light, having no part dark, the whole shall be full of light, as when the bright shining of a candle doth give thee light.

As Jesus spoke, a certain Pharisee besought him to dine with him: he went in, and sat down to meat. The Pharisee marvelled that Jesus had not washed before dinner.

The Lord said unto him,

Now do ye Pharisees make clean the outside of the cup and the platter; but your inward part is full of ravening and wickedness. Ye fools, did not he that made that which is without, make that which is within also? But rather give alms of such things as ye have; and, behold, all things are clean unto you.

But woe unto you, Pharisees! for ye tithe mint and rue and all manner of herbs, and pass over judgment and the love of God: these ought ye to have done, and not to leave the other undone.

Woe unto you, Pharisees! for ye love the uppermost seats in the synagogues, and greetings in the markets.

Woe unto you, scribes and Pharisees, hypocrites! for ye are as graves which appear not, and the men that walk over them are not aware of them.

Then answered one of the lawyers, Master, thus saying thou reproachest us also.

Jesus said,

Woe unto you also, ye lawyers! for ye lade men with burdens grievous to be borne, and ye yourselves touch not the burdens with one of your fingers.

Woe unto you! for ye build the sepulchres of the prophets, and your fathers killed them. Truly ye bear witness that ye allow the deeds of your fathers: for they indeed killed them, and ye build their sepulchres.

Therefore also said the wisdom of God, I will send them prophets and apostles, and some of them they shall slay and persecute: that the blood of all the prophets, which was shed from the foundation of the world, may be required of this generation; from the blood of Abel unto the blood of Zacharias, which perished between the altar and the temple: verily I say unto you, it shall be required of this generation.

Woe unto you, lawyers! for ye have taken away

the key of knowledge: ye entered not in yourselves,
and them that were entering in ye hindered.

As he said these things, the scribes and the Pharisees began to provoke him to speak of many things: laying wait for him, to catch something out of his mouth that they might accuse him.

Jesus preaches a sermon to the multitude

Luke 12:1–59; 13:1–9

In the meantime, when there were gathered together an innumerable multitude of people, insomuch that they trod one upon another, Jesus began to say unto his disciples first of all,

Beware ye of the leaven of the Pharisees, which is hypocrisy. For there is nothing covered that shall not be revealed; neither hid, that shall not be known. Therefore, whatsoever ye have spoken in darkness shall be heard in the light; and that which ye have spoken in the ear in closets shall be proclaimed upon the housetops.

And I say unto you, my friend, be not afraid of them that kill the body, and after that have no more that they can do. But I will forewarn you whom ye

shall fear: fear him, which after he hath killed hath power to cast into hell; yea, I say unto you, fear him.

Are not five sparrows sold for two farthings, and not one of them is forgotten before God? But even the very hairs on your head are all numbered. Fear not, therefore; ye are of more value than many sparrows.

Also I say unto you, whosoever shall confess me before men, him shall the Son of man also confess before the angels of God: but he that denieth me before men shall be denied before the angels of God. And whosoever shall speak a word against the Son of man, it shall be forgiven him: but unto him that blasphemeth against the Holy Ghost it shall not be forgiven.

And when they bring you unto the synagogues, and unto magistrates and powers, take ye no thought how or what thing ye shall answer, or what ye shall say: for the Holy Ghost shall teach you in the same hour what ye ought to say.

One of the company said, Master, speak to my brother, that he divide the inheritance with me.

Jesus answered,

Man, who made me a judge or a divider over you?

And he said unto them,

Take heed, and beware of covetousness: for a man's life consisteth not in the abundance of the things which he possesseth.

And he spake a parable:

The ground of a certain rich man brought forth

plentifully: and he thought within himself, saying, What shall I do, because I have no room where to bestow my fruits.

And he said, This will I do: I will pull down my barns, and build greater and there will I bestow all my fruits and my goods. And I will say to my soul, Soul, thou hast much goods laid up for many years; take thine ease, eat, drink and be merry.

But God said unto him, Thou fool, this night thy soul shall be required of thee: then whose shall those things be which thou hast provided?

So is he that layeth up treasure for himself, and is not rich towards God.

Jesus said unto his disciples,

Therefore I say unto you, take no thought for your life, what ye shall eat, neither for the body, what ye shall put on. The life is more than meat, and the body is more than raiment.

Consider the ravens: for they neither sow nor reap; which neither have storehouse nor barn; and God feedeth them: how much more are ye better than the fowls?

And which of you with taking thought can add to his stature one cubit? If ye then be not able to do that thing which is least, why take ye thought for the rest?

Consider the lilies how they grow: they toil not, they spin not; and yet I say unto you that Solomon in all his glory was not arrayed like one of these. If then God so clothe the grass, which is today in the field, and tomorrow is cast into the oven, how much more will he clothe you, O ye of little faith?

And seek not ye what ye shall eat, or what ye shall drink, neither be ye of doubtful mind. For all these things do the nations of the world seek after; and your Father knoweth that ye have need of these things.

But rather seek ye the kingdom of God; and all these things shall be added unto you.

Fear not, little flock; for it is your Father's good pleasure to give you the kingdom. Sell that ye have, and give alms; provide yourselves bags which wax not old, a treasure in the heavens that faileth not, where no thief approacheth, neither moth corrupteth. For where your treasure is, there will your heart be also.

Let your loins be girded about, and your lights burning; and ye yourselves like unto men that wait for their lord, when he will return from the

wedding; that when he cometh and knocketh, they
may open unto him immediately.

Blessed are those servants whom the lord when
he cometh shall find watching: verily I say unto you
that he shall gird himself, and make them to sit
down to meat, and will come forth and serve them.
And if he shall come in the second watch, or come
in the third watch, and find them so, blessed are
those servants. And this know, that if the goodman
of the house had known what hour the thief would
come, he would have watched and not have
suffered his house to be broken through. Be ye
therefore ready also; for the Son of man cometh at
an hour when ye think not.

Then Peter said, Lord, speakest thou this parable unto us, or
even to all?

The Lord said,

Who then is that faithful and wise steward, whom his lord shall make ruler over his household, to give them their portion of meat in due season?

Blessed is that servant, whom his lord when he cometh shall find so doing. Of a truth I say unto you that he will make him ruler over all that he hath.

But if that servant say in his heart, My lord delayeth his coming; and shall begin to beat the menservants and maidens, and to eat and drink, and to be drunken; the lord of that servant will come in a day when he looketh not for him, and at an hour when he is not aware, and will cut him in sunder, and will appoint him his portion with the unbelievers.

And that servant, which knew his lord's will, and prepared not himself, neither did according to his will, shall be beaten with many stripes. But he that knew not, and did commit things worthy of stripes, shall be beaten with few stripes. For unto whomsoever much is given, of him shall be much required; and to whom men have committeth much, of him they will ask more.

I am come to send fire on the earth; and what will I, if it be already kindled? But I have a baptism to be baptized with; and how am I straitened till it be accomplished!

Suppose ye that I am come to give peace on earth? I tell you, nay; but rather division: for from henceforth there shall be five in one house divided, three against two, and two against three. The father shall be divided against the son, and the son against the father; the mother against the daughter, and the daughter against the mother; the mother-in-law against her daughter-in-law, and the daughter-in-law against her mother-in-law.

He said also to the people,

When ye see a cloud rise out of the west, straightway ye say, There cometh a shower and so it is. And when ye see the south wind blow, ye say, There will be heat; and it cometh to pass. Ye hypocrites, ye can discern the face of the sky and of the earth: but how is it that ye do not discern this time? Yea, and why even of yourselves judge ye not what is right?

When thou goest with thine adversary to the magistrate, as thou art in the way, give diligence that thou mayest be delivered from him; lest he hale thee to the judge, and the judge deliver thee to the officer, and the officer cast thee into prison. I tell thee, thou shalt not depart thence till thou hast paid the very last mite.

There were present at that season some that told him of the Galileans, whose blood Pilate had mingled with their sacrifices. Jesus said unto them,

Suppose ye that these Galileans were sinners above all Galileans, because they suffered such things? I tell you, nay: but, except ye repent, ye shall all likewise perish.

Or those eighteen, upon whom the tower in Siloam fell and slew them, think ye that they were sinners above all men that dwelt in Jerusalem? I tell you, nay: but, except ye repent, ye shall all likewise perish.

He spake also this parable:

A certain man had a fig tree planted in his vineyard; and he came and sought fruit thereon, and found none. Then said he unto the dresser of

his vineyard, Behold, these three years I come seeking fruit on this fig tree, and find none: cut it down; why cumbereth it the ground?

And he answering said unto him, Lord, let it alone this year also, till I shall dig about it, and dung it: and if it bear fruit, well: and if not, then after that thou shalt cut it down.

Sabbath cure

Luke 13:10–21

Jesus was teaching in one of the synagogues on the sabbath. And, behold, there was a woman which had a spirit of infirmity eighteen years, and was bowed together, and could in no wise lift up herself. Jesus saw her, and said unto her,

Woman, thou are loosed from thine infirmity.

He laid his hands on her: and immediately she was made straight.

The ruler of the synagogue said with indignation unto the people, There are six days in which men ought to work: in them therefore come and be healed, but not on the sabbath day.

The Lord answered,

Thou hypocrite, doth not each one of you on the sabbath loose his ox or his ass from the stall, and lead him away to watering? And ought not this woman, being a daughter of Abraham, whom Satan

hath bound, lo, these eighteen years, be loosed from
this bond on the sabbath day?

His adversaries were ashamed: and the people rejoiced for the glorious things that were done by him.
Then said he,

Unto what is the kingdom of God like? and
whereunto shall I resemble it? It is like a grain of
mustard seed, which a man took, and cast into his
garden; and it grew, and waxed a great tree; and
the fowls of the air lodged in the branches of it.

And again he said,

Whereunto shall l liken the kingdom of God? It is
like leaven, which a woman took and hid in three
measures of meal, till the whole was leavened.

Journeying towards Jerusalem

Luke 13:22–35; 10:38–42; John 10:39–40

Jesus went through the cities and villages, teaching and journeying towards Jerusalem.

One said unto him, Lord, are there few that be saved?

And he said,

Strive to enter in at the strait gate: for many, I say unto you, will seek to enter in, and shall not be able.

When once the master of the house is risen up, and hath shut the door, then are ye made to stand without, and to knock at the door, saying, Lord, Lord, open unto us: and he shall answer and say unto you, I know you not whence ye are. Then shall ye begin to say, We have eaten and drunk in thy presence, and thou hast taught in our streets.

But he shall say, I tell you, I know you not whence ye are; depart from me, all ye workers of iniquity.

There shall be weeping and gnashing of teeth when ye shall see Abraham, and Isaac, and Jacob, and all the prophets, in the kingdom of God, and you yourselves thrust out.

And they shall come from the east, and from the west, and from the north, and from the south, and shall sit down in the kingdom of God.

And, behold, there are last which shall be first; and there are first which shall be last.

The same day there came Pharisees saying unto Jesus, Depart hence for Herod will kill thee.

And he said unto them,

Go ye, and tell that fox, Behold, I cast out devils, and I do cures today and tomorrow, and the third day I shall be perfected. Nevertheless, I must walk today, and tomorrow, and the day following: for it cannot be that a prophet perish out of Jerusalem.

O Jerusalem, Jerusalem, which killest the prophets, and stonest them that are sent unto thee; how often would I have gathered thy children together, as a hen doth gather her brood under her wings, and ye would not! Behold, your house is left unto you desolate: and verily I say unto you, ye shall not see me, until the time come when ye shall say, Blessed is he that cometh in the name of the Lord.

Now it came to pass, as they went, that Jesus entered into a certain village and a woman named Martha received him into her house. She had a sister, Mary, which sat at Jesus's feet, and heard his word.

But Martha, cumbered about much serving, said, Lord, dost

thou not care that my sister hath left me to serve alone? Bid her that she help me.

Jesus answered,

Martha, Martha, thou are careful and troubled about many things: but one thing is needful; and Mary hath chosen that good part, which shall not be taken away from her.

The Jews sought again to take Jesus: but he went away beyond Jordan into the place where John at first baptized; and he abode there.

Sabbath healing and preaching

Luke 14:1–35

On a sabbath day, as Jesus went into the house of one of the chief Pharisees to eat bread, they watched him. And, behold, there was a man which had the dropsy. And Jesus spoke to the lawyers and Pharisees, saying,

Is it lawful to heal on the sabbath day?

They held their peace. Jesus healed the man, and let him go, saying unto them,

Which of you shall have an ass or an ox fallen into a pit, and will not straightway pull him out on the sabbath day?

They could not answer him.

To those which were bidden, when he marked how they chose out the chief rooms, he put forth a parable, saying,

When thou are bidden of any man to a wedding, sit not down in the highest room, lest a more honourable man than thou be bidden of him, and he that bade thee come and say to thee, Give this man place; and thou begin with shame to take the lowest room.

But when thou are bidden, go and sit down in the lowest room; that when he that bade thee cometh, he may say unto thee, Friend, go up higher: then shalt thou have worship in the presence of them that sit at meat with thee.

For whosoever exalteth himself shall be abased; and he that humbleth himself shall be exalted.

Then said he to the Pharisee that bade him,

When thou makest a dinner or a supper, call not thy friends, nor thy brethren, neither thy kinsmen, nor thy rich neighbours; lest they also bid thee again, and a recompense be made thee. But when thou makest a feast, call the poor, the maimed, the lame, the blind; and thou shalt be blessed; for they cannot recompense thee: for thou shalt be recompensed at the resurrection of the just.

One of them that sat at meat with Jesus said unto him, Blessed is he that shall eat bread in the kingdom of God.

Then said Jesus,

A certain man made a great supper, and bade many: and sent his servant at suppertime to say to them that were bidden, Come; for all things are now ready. And they all with one consent began to make excuse.

The first said unto him, I have bought a piece of ground, and I must needs go and see it: I pray thee have me excused. And another said, I have bought five yoke of oxen, and I go to prove them: I pray thee have me excused. And another said, I have married a wife, and therefore I cannot come.

So that servant came and showed his lord these things. Then the master of the house being angry said to his servant, Go out quickly into the streets and lanes of the city, and bring in hither the poor, and the maimed, and the halt, and the blind.

And the servant said, Lord, it is done as thou hast commanded, and yet there is room.

And the lord said unto the servant, Go out into the highways and hedges, and compel them to come in, that my house may be filled. For I say unto you that none of those men which were bidden shall taste of my supper.

There went multitudes with Jesus: and he turned, and said unto them,

If any man come to me, and hate not his father, and mother, and wife, and children, and brethren, and sisters, yea, and his own life also, he cannot be my disciple. And whosoever doth not bear his cross, and come after me, cannot be my disciple.

For which of you, intending to build a tower, sitteth not down first and counteth the cost, whether he have sufficient to finish it? Lest haply, after he hath laid the foundation, and is not able to finish it, all that behold it begin to mock him. saying, This man began to build, and was not able to finish

Or what king, going to make war against another king, sitteth not down first and consulteth whether he be able with ten thousand to meet him

that cometh against him with twenty thousand? Or else, while the other is yet a great way off, he sendeth an ambassage and desireth conditions of peace. So likewise, whosoever he be of you that forsaketh not all that he hath, he cannot be my disciple.

Salt is good: but if the salt have lost its savour, wherewith shall it be seasoned? It is neither fit for the land, nor yet for the dunghill, and men cast it out. He that hath ears to hear, let him hear.

The parables of the lost sheep, the piece of silver and the prodigal son

Luke 15, 1–32

Then drew near unto Jesus the publicans and sinners for to hear him. The Pharisees and scribes murmured, This man receiveth sinners, and eateth with them.

Jesus spake this parable unto them,

What man of you, having a hundred sheep, if he lose one of them, doth not leave the ninety and nine in the wilderness, and go after that which is lost, until he find it? And when he hath found it, he layeth it on his shoulders, rejoicing. And when he cometh home, he calleth together his friends and neighbours, saying unto them, Rejoice with me, for I have found my sheep which was lost.

I say unto you that, likewise, joy shall be in

heaven over one sinner that repenteth, more than over ninety and nine just persons, which need no repentance.

What woman, having ten pieces of silver, if she lose one piece, doth not light a candle, and sweep the house, and seek diligently till she find it? And when she hath found it, she calleth her friends and her neighbours together, saying, Rejoice with me: for I have found the piece which I had lost.

Likewise, I say unto you, there is joy in the presence of the angels of God over one sinner that repenteth.

A certain man had two sons and the younger of them said to his father, Father, give me the portion of goods that falleth to me. And he divided unto them his living.

And not many days after, the younger son

gathered all together, and took his journey into a far country, and there wasted his substance with riotous living. And when he had spent all, there arose a mighty famine in that land; and he began to be in want.

And he went and joined himself to a citizen of that country; and he sent him into his fields to feed swine. And he would fain have filled his belly with the husks that the swine did eat; and no man gave unto him.

And when he came to himself, he said, How many hired servants of my father's have bread enough and to spare, and I perish with hunger! I will arise and go to my father, and will say unto him, Father, I have sinned against heaven, and before thee, and am no more worthy to be called thy son: make me as one of thy hired servants.

And he arose, and came to his father. But when he was yet a great way off, his father saw him, and had compassion, and ran, and fell on his neck, and kissed him.

And the son said unto him, Father, I have sinned against heaven, and in thy sight, and am no more worthy to be called thy son.

But the father said to his servants, Bring forth the best robe, and put it on him; and put a ring on his hand, and shoes on his feet: and bring hither the fatted calf, and kill it; and let us eat, and be merry: for this my son was dead, and is alive again; he was lost, and is found. And they began to be merry.

Now his elder son was in the field: and as he came and drew nigh to the house, he heard music and dancing. And he called one of the servants, and asked what these things meant. And he said unto him, Thy brother is come, and thy father hath killed the fatted calf, because he hath received him safe and sound. And he was angry, and would not go in: therefore came his father out, and entreated him.

And he answering said to his father, Lo, these many years do I serve thee, neither transgressed I at any time thy commandment; and yet thou never gavest me a kid, that I might make merry with my friends: but as soon as this thy son was come, which hath devoured thy living with harlots, thou hast killed for him the fatted calf.

And he said unto him, Son, thou art ever with me and all that I have is thine. It was meet that we should make merry, and be glad: for this thy brother was dead, and is alive again; and was lost, and is found.

The parables of the unjust steward and of the rich man and Lazarus

Luke 16:1–31

Jesus said also to his disciples,

There was a certain rich man, which had a steward; and the same was accused unto him that he had wasted his goods. And he called him, and said unto him, How is it that I hear this of thee? give an account of thy stewardship; for thou mayest be no longer steward.

Then the steward said within himself, What shall I do? for my lord taketh away from me the stewardship: I cannot dig: to beg I am ashamed. I am resolved what to do, that, when I am put out of the stewardship, they may receive me into their houses.

So he called every one of his lord's debtors unto him, and said unto the first, How much owest thou unto my lord? And he said, A hundred measures of oil. And he said unto him, Take thy bill, and sit down quickly, and write fifty.

Then said he to another, And how much owest thou? And he said, A hundred measures of wheat. And he said unto him, Take thy bill, and write four-score.

And the lord commended the unjust steward, because he had done wisely: for the children of this world are in their generation wiser than the children of light.

And I say unto you, Make to yourselves friends of the mammon of unrighteousness; that, when ye fail, they may receive you into everlasting habitations.

He that is faithful in that which is least is faithful also in much: and he that is unjust in the least is unjust also in much.

If therefore ye have not been faithful in the unrighteous mammon, who will commit to your trust the true riches? And if ye have not been faithful in that which is another man's, who shall give you that which is your own?

No servant can serve two masters: for either he will hate the one and love the other, or else he will hold to the one and despise the other. Ye cannot serve God and mammon.

The Pharisees, who were covetous, also heard all these things: and they derided Jesus.

He said to them,

Ye are they which justify yourselves before men; but

God knoweth your hearts: for that which is highly esteemed among men is abomination in the sight of God. The law and the prophets were until John: since that time the kingdom of God is preached, and every man presseth into it. And it is easier for heaven and earth to pass, than one tittle of the law to fail.

Whosoever putteth away his wife, and marrieth another, committeth adultery; and whosoever marrieth her that is put away from her husband committeth adultery.

There was a certain rich man, which was clothed in purple and fine linen, and fared sumptuously every day: and there was a certain beggar named Lazarus, which was laid at his gate, full of sores, and desiring to be fed with the crumbs which fell from the rich man's table: moreover the dogs came and licked his sores.

And it came to pass that the beggar died, and was carried by the angels into Abraham's bosom: the rich man also died and was buried; and in hell he lifted up his eyes, being in torments, and seeth Abraham afar off, and Lazarus in his bosom. And he cried and said, Father Abraham, have mercy on me, and send Lazarus, that he may dip the tip of his finger in water and cool my tongue: for I am tormented in this flame.

But Abraham said, Son, remember that thou in thy lifetime receivedst thy good things, and likewise Lazarus evil things: but now he is comforted and thou art tormented. And beside all this, between us and you there is a great gulf fixed: so that they which would pass from hence to you cannot; neither can they pass to us, that would come from thence.

Then he said, I pray thee therefore, father, that thou wouldest send him to my father's house: for I have five brethren, and there he may testify unto them, lest they also come into this place of torment.

Abraham saith unto him, They have Moses and the prophets; let them hear them.

And he said, Nay, father Abraham: but if one went unto them from the dead, they will repent.

And he said unto him, If they hear not Moses and the prophets, neither will they be persuaded, though one rose from the dead.

Lazarus is raised from the dead

Luke 17:1–10; John 11:1–54

Then said Jesus unto the disciples,

It is impossible but that offences will come: but woe unto him through whom they come! It were better for him that a millstone were hanged about his neck, and he cast into the sea, than that he should offend one of these little ones.

Take heed to yourselves: If thy brother trespass against thee, rebuke him; and if he repent, forgive him. And if he trespass against thee seven times in a day, and seven times in a day turn again to thee, saying, I repent; thou shalt forgive him.

The apostles said unto the Lord, Increase our faith.
And the Lord said,

If ye had faith as a grain of mustard seed, ye might say unto this sycamine tree, Be thou plucked up by the root, and be thou planted in the sea; and it should obey you.

But which of you, having a servant ploughing or feeding cattle, will say unto him by and by, when he is come from the field, Go and sit down to meat? and will not rather say unto him, Make ready wherewith I may sup, and gird thyself, and serve me, till I have eaten and drunken; and afterward thou shalt eat and drink?

Doth he thank that servant because he did the things that were commanded him? I trow not.

So likewise ye, when ye shall have done all those things which are commanded you, say, We are unprofitable servants: we have done that which was our duty to do.

Now it happened that Lazarus, of Bethany, the brother of Mary and Martha, was sick. (It was that Mary which anointed the Lord with ointment, and wiped his feet with her hair.) The sisters sent unto Jesus, saying, Lord, behold, he whom thou lovest is sick.

Jesus said,

This sickness is not unto death, but for the glory of God, that the Son of God might be glorified thereby.

Now Jesus loved Martha, and her sister, and Lazarus. He abode two days in the place where he was, then said he to his disciples,

Let us go into Judea again.

His disciples say, Master, the Jews of late sought to stone thee, and goest thou thither again?

Jesus answered,

Are there not twelve hours in the day? If any man walk in the day, he stumbleth not, because he seeth

the light of this world. But if a man walk in the night, he stumbleth, because there is no light in him.

Our friend Lazarus sleepeth; but I go, that I may awake him out of sleep.

Jesus spoke of Lazarus's death; but they thought that he had spoken of rest in sleep. Then he said plainly,

Lazarus is dead. And I am glad for your sakes that I was not there, to the intent ye may believe; nevertheless let us go unto him.

And when Jesus came, he found that Lazarus had lain in the grave four days.

Martha, as soon as she heard that Jesus was coming, went and met him; but Mary was still in the house. Then said Martha unto Jesus, Lord, if thou hadst been here, my brother had not died. But I know that even now, whatsoever thou wilt ask of God, God will give it thee.

Jesus replied,

Thy brother shall rise again.

Martha answered, I know that he shall rise again in the resurrection at the last day.

Jesus said unto her,

I am the resurrection, and the life; he that believeth in me, though he were dead, yet shall he live: and whosoever liveth and believeth in me shall never die. Believest thou this?

Martha saith, Yea, Lord: I believe that thou art the Christ, the Son of God, which should come into the world.

When she had so said, she went her way, and called Mary her sister secretly, saying, The Master is come, and calleth for thee.

Mary arose quickly, and came unto him in that place where Martha had met him. The Jews which were with Mary in the house followed her. She fell at Jesus's feet, saying, Lord, if thou hadst been here, my brother had not died.

Jesus saw her weeping; he groaned in the spirit and was troubled and asked,

Where have ye laid him?

They said, Lord, come and see.
Jesus wept.
Then said the Jews, Behold how he loved him!
Jesus came to the grave. It was a cave, and a stone lay upon it. Jesus said,

Take ye away the stone.

Martha, the sister, saith, Lord, he hath been dead four days. Jesus said.

Said I not unto thee that, if thou wouldst believe, thou shouldst see the glory of God?

Then they took away the stone. And Jesus lifted up his eyes, and said,

Father, I thank thee that thou hast heard me. And I knew that thou hearest me always: but because of the people which stand by I said it that they may believe that thou hast sent me.

When he had thus spoken, he cried,

Lazarus, come forth.

He that was dead came forth. bound with graveclothes. Jesus said,

Loose him, and let him go.

Then gathered the chief priests and the Pharisees a council, and said, What do we? for this man doeth many miracles. If we let him alone, all men will believe on him: and the Romans shall come and take away both our place and nation.

From that day forth they conspired to put Jesus to death. Jesus therefore walked no more openly among the Jews.

One grateful Samaritan

Luke 17:11–37; 18:1–8

As Jesus went to Jerusalem, he passed through Samaria and Galilee. In a certain village ten lepers, which stood far off, lifted up their voices, and said, Jesus, Master, have mercy on us.

He said unto them,

Go show yourselves unto the priests.

As they went, they were cleansed. And one of them turned back, and fell at Jesus's feet, giving him thanks: he was a Samaritan.

Jesus said,

Were there not ten cleansed? but where are the nine? There are not found that returned to give glory to God, save this stranger.

And he said to the Samaritan,

Arise, go thy way: thy faith hath made thee whole.

When Jesus was demanded of the Pharisees when the kingdom of God should come, he answered,

The kingdom of God cometh not with observation; neither shall they say, Lo here! or, Lo there! for, behold, the kingdom of God is within you.

And he said unto his disciples,

The days will come when ye shall desire to see one of the days of the Son of man, and ye shall not see it. And they shall say to you, See here; or, See there: go not after them, nor follow them. For as the lightning, that lighteneth out of the one part under heaven, shineth unto the other part under heaven, so shall also the Son of man be in his day.

But first must he suffer many things, and be rejected of this generation.

And as it was in the days of Noe, so shall it be also in the days of the Son of man. They did eat, they drank, they married wives, they were given in marriage, until the day that Noe entered into the ark, and the flood came, and destroyed them all.

Likewise also as it was in the days of Lot; they did eat, they drank, they bought, they sold, they planted, they built; but the same day that Lot went out of Sodom it rained fire and brimstone from heaven, and destroyed them all.

Even thus shall it be in the day when the Son of man is revealed. In that day, he which shall be upon the housetop, and his stuff in the house, let him not come down to take it away; and he that is in the field, let him likewise not return back.

Remember Lot's wife.

Whosoever shall seek to save his life shall lose it;

and whosoever shall lose his life shall preserve it.

I tell you, in that night there shall be two men in one bed; the one shall be taken and the other shall be left. Two women shall be grinding together; the one shall be taken and the other left. Two men shall be in the field; the one shall be taken and the other left.

They said unto Jesus, Where, Lord?
He answered,

Wheresoever the body is, thither will the eagles be gathered together.

He urged men always to pray, and not to faint, saying,

There was in a city a judge, which feared not God neither regarded man; and there was a widow in that city, and she came unto him, saying, Avenge me of mine adversary.

And he would not for a while: but afterward he said within himself, Though I fear not God, nor regard man, yet because this widow troubleth me, I will avenge her, lest by her continual coming she weary me.

And the Lord said,

Hear what the unjust judge saith. And shall not God avenge his own elect, which cry day and night unto him, though he bear long with them? I tell you that he will avenge them speedily. Nevertheless, when the Son of man cometh, shall he find faith on the earth?

Jesus continues to speak in parables

Luke 18:9–30; Mark 10:13–31; Matthew 19:13–30; 20:1–16

Jesus spake this parable unto certain which trusted in themselves that they were righteous, and despised others:

Two men went up into the temple to pray; the one a Pharisee and the other a publican.

The Pharisee stood and prayed thus with himself: God, I thank thee that I am not as other men are, extortioners, unjust, adulterers, or even as this publican. I fast twice in the week, I give tithes of all that I possess.

And the publican, standing afar off, would not lift up so much as his eyes unto heaven, but smote upon his breast, saying, God be merciful to me a sinner.

I tell you, this man went down to his house

justified rather than the other: for every man that exalteth himself shall be abased; and he that humbleth himself shall be exalted.

Then were brought infants, that Jesus should touch them: but the disciples rebuked them that brought them.

Jesus, much displeased, said unto the disciples,

Suffer the little children to come unto me, and forbid them not: for of such is the kingdom of heaven. Verily I say unto you, whosoever shall not receive the kingdom of God as a little child, he shall in no wise enter therein.

He took them up in his arms, put his hands upon them, and blessed them; and he departed thence.

When he was gone forth into the way there came one running, a ruler, and kneeled, and asked, Good Master what shall I do to inherit eternal life?

Jesus answered,

Why callest thou me good? None is good, save one, that is God, but if thou wilt enter into life, keep the commandments.

Thou knowest the commandments: Do not commit adultery; Do not kill; Do not steal; Do not bear false witness; Defraud not; Honour thy father and thy mother; Love thy neighbour as thyself.

The young man saith, All these things have I kept from my youth up: what lack I yet?

Jesus beholding him loved him, and said,

Yet lackest thou one thing; if thou wilt be perfect, go thy way, sell all that thou hast, and distribute unto the poor, and thou shalt have treasure in heaven: and come, take up the cross and follow me.

The young man went away grieved, for he was rich and had great possessions.

Jesus looked round about, and saith,

How hardly shall they that have riches enter into the kingdom of God? It is easier for a camel to go through the eye of a needle, than for a rich man to enter into the kingdom of God.

The disciples were amazed at his words. But Jesus said again,

Children, how hard is it for them that trust in riches to enter into the kingdom of God! Verily I say unto you that a rich man shall hardly enter into the kingdom of heaven! And again I say unto you, it is easier for a camel to go through a needle's eye than for a rich man to enter into the kingdom of God.

The disciples were saying among themselves, Who then can be saved?

And Jesus answered,

With men this is impossible; but not with God. The things which are impossible with men are possible with God: for with God all things are possible.

Then Peter said, Lo, we have left all, and have followed thee. What shall we have therefore?
Jesus saith,

Ye which have followed me, in the regeneration when the Son of man shall sit in the throne of his glory, ye also shall sit upon twelve thrones, judging the twelve tribes of Israel.

There is not a man that hath forsaken houses, or father, or mother, or brethren, or sisters, or wife, or children, or lands, for the kingdom of God's sake, for my sake and the gospel's, but he shall receive a hundredfold, and shall inherit everlasting life.

Verily I say unto you, everyone that hath left

house, or father, or mother, or brethren, or sisters, or wife, or children, or lands, for my name's sake and the gospel's, shall receive manifold more in this present time, with persecutions besides; and shall inherit life everlasting in the world to come.

But many that are first shall be last; and the last shall be first.

For the kingdom of heaven is like unto a man that is a householder which went out early in the morning to hire labourers into his vineyard. And when he had agreed with the labourers for a penny a day, he sent them into his vineyard.

And he went out about the third hour, and saw others standing idle in the marketplace, and said unto them, Go ye also into the vineyard, and whatsoever is right I will give you. And they went their way.

Again he went out about the sixth and ninth hour and did likewise.

And about the eleventh hour he went out, and found others standing idle, and saith unto them, Why stand ye here all the day idle? They say unto him, Because no man hath hired us. He saith unto them, Go ye also into the vineyard; and whatsoever is right, that shall ye receive.

So when even was come, the lord of the vineyard saith unto his steward, Call the labourers, and give them their hire, beginning from the last unto the first.

And when they came that were hired about the eleventh hour, they received every man a penny.

So when the first came, they supposed that they should receive more; but they likewise received every man a penny. And when they had received it, they murmured against the goodman of the house, saying, These last have wrought but one hour, and thou hast made them equal unto us, which have borne the burden and heat of the day.

But he answered one of them, and said, Friend, I do thee no wrong: didst not thou agree with me for a penny? Take that thine is, and go thy way: I will give unto this last, even as unto thee. Is it not lawful for me to do what I will with mine own? Is thine eye evil, because I am good?

So the last shall be first, and the first last; for many be called, but few chosen.

The question of divorce

Mark 10:1–12; Matthew 19:1–12

Into the coasts of Judea by the farther side of Jordan, multitudes followed Jesus and, as he was wont, he taught them.

The Pharisees, tempting him, asked Jesus, Is it lawful for a man to put away his wife for every cause?

He answered.

What did Moses command you?

They said, Moses suffered to write a bill of divorcement, and to put her away.

Jesus answered,

For the hardness of your heart he wrote you his precept. But from the beginning of creation God made them male and female. For this cause shall a man leave his father and mother, and cleave to his wife.

Have ye not read, that he which made them at the beginning made them male and female, and said, For this cause shall man leave father and mother, and shall cleave to his wife: and they twain shall be one flesh? What therefore God hath joined together, let no man put asunder.

They asked, Why did Moses then command to give a writing of divorcement and to put her away?
He told them,

Moses, because of the hardness of your hearts, suffered you to put away your wives: but from the beginning it was not so. And I say unto you, whosoever shall put away his wife, except it be for fornication, and shall marry another, committeth adultery: and whoso marrieth her which is put away doth commit adultery.

In the house his disciples asked Jesus again of the same matter. He said,

Whosoever shall put away his wife, and marry another, committeth adultery against her. And if a woman shall put away her husband, and be married to another, she committeth adultery.

The disciples said to him, If the case of the man be so with his wife, it is not good to marry.

But Jesus answered,

All men cannot receive this saying, save they to whom it is given. For there are some eunuchs which were so born from their mother's womb: and there are some eunuchs which were made eunuchs of men: and there be eunuchs which have made themselves eunuchs for the kingdom of heaven's sake.

He that is able to receive it, let him receive it.

Jesus speaks of imminent betrayal and answers James and John

Matthew 20:17–28; Mark 10:32–45; Luke 18:31–34

On the way up to Jerusalem, Jesus took the disciples aside and began to tell them what things were going to happen to him, saying,

> *Behold, we go up to Jerusalem; and the Son of man shall be betrayed and delivered unto the chief priests, and unto the scribes; and they shall condemn him to death, and shall deliver him unto the Gentiles to be spitefully entreated and spat upon.*
>
> *They shall mock him, and shall scourge him, and shall crucify and kill him; and the third day he shall rise again.*
>
> *And all the things that are written by the*

prophets concerning the Son of man shall be accomplished.

They twelve disciples understood none of the things which were spoken.

Then came unto Jesus the mother of James and John, the sons of Zebedee, desiring a certain thing of him. He said unto her,

What wilt thou?

And he said to the sons,

What would ye that I should do for you?

She saith, Grant that these my two sons may sit, the one on thy right hand and the other on thy left, in glory in thy kingdom.

But Jesus said unto them,

Ye know not what ye ask: are ye able to drink of the cup that I shall drink of, and to be baptized with the baptism that I am baptized with?

And they replied, We can.
Jesus answered,

Ye shall drink indeed of my cup, the cup that I drink of: and with the baptism that I am baptized withal ye shall be baptized: but to sit on my right hand and on my left hand is not mine to give, but it shall be given to them for whom it is prepared of my Father.

The ten were moved with indignation against the two brethren.
But Jesus called them to him, and said,

Ye know that the princes of the Gentiles exercise dominion over them; ye know that they which are accounted to rule over the Gentiles exercise lordship over them; and their great ones exercise authority upon them.

But so shall it not be among you: but whosoever will be great among you, shall be your minister: and whosoever of you will be the chiefest, shall be servant of all: let him be your servant, even as the Son of man: for even the Son of man came not to be ministered unto, but to minister, and to give his life a ransom for many.

Jesus passes through Jericho

Luke 18:35–43; 19:1–27; Mark 10:46–52

A multitude followed Jesus. Nigh unto Jericho, a certain blind man sat by the wayside begging: and hearing the multitude, he asked what it meant. They told him, Jesus of Nazareth passeth by.

And he cried, Jesus, thou Son of David, have mercy on me.

Jesus commanded him to be brought, and asked him,

What wilt thou that I shall do unto thee?

And he said, Lord, that I may receive my sight.

Jesus said unto him,

Receive thy sight: thy faith hath saved thee.

Immediately he received his sight, and forthwith he followed Jesus, glorifying God.

Jesus entered and passed through Jericho, and as he left the city with his disciples, he passed blind Bartimeus sitting at the side of the highway begging. When he heard that it was Jesus of

Nazareth, he began to cry out, Jesus, Son of David, have mercy on me.

Many charged him that he should hold his peace: but he cried the more, Thou Son of David, have mercy on me.

Jesus commanded him to be called, and they told him, Be of good comfort; he calleth thee.

Casting away his garment, he came to Jesus, who asked him,

What wilt thou that I shall do unto thee?

The blind man said, Lord, that I might receive my sight.
And Jesus said,

Go thy way; thy faith hath made thee whole.

Immediately his eyes received sight, and he also followed Jesus in the way.

When Jesus was passing through Jericho, a man named Zaccheus, a rich and notable publican, sought to see Jesus and could not for the press, because he was little of stature. He ran before, and climbed into a sycamore tree to see Jesus: for he was to pass that way.

When Jesus came to the place he looked up, and saw Zaccheus, and said,

Zaccheus, make haste and come down: for today I must abide at thy house.

He came down and received Jesus joyfully. When they saw it they murmured, He is gone to be guest with a man that is a sinner.

Zaccheus said unto the Lord: Behold, the half of my goods I give to the poor; and if I have taken anything from any man by false accusation, I restore him fourfold.

Jesus said,

This day is salvation come to this house, forsomuch as he also is a son of Abraham. For the Son of man is come to seek and to save that which was lost.

And he added a parable, because he was nigh to Jerusalem, and they thought that the kingdom of God should immediately appear. He said therefore,

A certain nobleman went into a far country to receive for himself a kingdom, and to return. And he called his ten servants, and delivered each a pound, and said unto them, Occupy till I come.

But his citizens hated him, and sent a message after him, saying, We will not have this man to reign over us.

And it came to pass, that when he was returned, having received the kingdom, then he commanded these servants to be called unto him, to whom he had given the money, that he might know how much every man had gained by trading.

Then came the first saying, Lord, thy pound hath gained ten pounds. And he said unto him, Well, thou good servant: because thou hast been faithful in a very little, have thou authority over ten cities.

And the second came, saying, Lord, thy pound

hath gained five pounds. And he said likewise to him, Be thou also over five cities.

And another came, saying, Lord, behold, here is thy pound, which I have kept laid up in a napkin; for I feared thee because thou art an austere man: thou takest up that thou layest not down and reapest that thou didst not sow.

And he saith unto him, Out of thine own mouth will I judge thee, thou wicked servant. Thou knewest that I was an austere man, taking up that I laid not down, and reaping that I did not sow: wherefore then gavest not thou my money into the bank, that at my coming I might have required mine own with usury?

And he said unto them that stood by, Take from him the pound, and give it to him that hath ten pounds. (And they said unto him, Lord, he hath ten pounds.) And those mine enemies, which would not that I should reign over them, bring hither, and slay them before me.

For I say unto you that unto everyone which hath shall be given; and from him that hath not, even that he hath shall be taken away from him.

Christ's entry into Jerusalem

John 11:55–57; Matthew 21:1–6; Mark 11:1–11; Luke 19:28–44

The Jews' Passover was at hand; and many went out of the country up to Jerusalem to purify themselves. Jesus went before, ascending up to Jerusalem.

Now the chief priests and the Pharisees had given a commandment that if any man knew where Jesus was, he should show it that they might take him.

When Jesus came to Bethphage and Bethany, at the Mount of Olives, nigh unto Jerusalem, he sent forth two disciples, saying,

Go ye your way into the village over against you, in the which, as soon as ye be entered into it, straightway ye shall find an ass tied, and a colt with her, whereon yet never man sat; loose them, and bring them hither unto me.

And if any man say aught unto you, and ask you, Why do ye this? why do ye loose them? ye shall say,

Because the Lord hath need of them; and straightway he will send them hither.

The disciples went, and did as Jesus had commanded. The owners said, Why loose ye them? They answered, The Lord hath need of them. And they let them go.

They brought the ass and the colt, and put their garments on the colt; and they set Jesus thereon.

As he went, many spread their clothes in the way; and others cut branches off the trees, and strewed them in the way.

At the descent of the Mount of Olives, the multitude began to praise God saying, Hosanna to the Son of David! Blessed be the King that cometh in the name of the Lord. Hosanna in the highest: peace in heaven!

Some of the Pharisees said unto Jesus. Master, rebuke thy disciples.

He answered,

I tell you that if these should hold their peace, the stones would immediately cry out.

When Jesus was come near, he beheld the city, and wept over it, saying,

If thou hadst known, even thou, at least in this thy day, the things which belong unto thy peace! but now they are hid from thine eyes.

For the days shall come upon thee that thine enemies shall cast a trench about thee, and compass thee round, and keep thee in on every side. And shall lay thee even with the ground, and thy children within thee; and they shall not leave in thee one stone upon another; because thou knewest not the time of thy visitation.

When Jesus was come into Jerusalem, he taught in the temple. All the city was moved. The blind and the lame came to him, and he healed them.

The wonderful things that he did, and the children crying in the temple Hosanna to the Son of David, displeased the chief priests and the scribes and they said unto Jesus, Hearest thou what these say?

He answered,

Yea; have ye never read, Out of the mouth of babes and sucklings thou hast perfected praise?

And when he had looked round about upon all things, the eventide being come, he went out with the twelve unto Bethany, and lodged there.

The withering of the fig tree and the purging of the temple

Mark 11:12–26; Matthew 21:12–13, 18–22; Luke 19, 45–48

Now in the morning, as Jesus returned into the city, he was hungry: and seeing afar off a fig tree, he came to it, but found nothing but leaves, for the time of the figs was not yet. And he said,

Let no fruit grow on thee henceforward. No man eat fruit of thee hereafter for ever.

Presently the fig tree withered away. The disciples saw it and said, How soon is the fig tree withered away!

Jesus answered,

Verily I say unto you, if ye have faith, and doubt not, ye shall not only do this which is done to the fig tree, but also if ye shall say to this mountain, Be thou removed, and be thou cast into the sea; it shall

be done. And all things, whatsoever ye shall ask in
prayer, believing, ye shall receive.

They came to Jerusalem, and Jesus went into the temple, and began to cast out them that sold and bought therein, and overthrew the tables of the moneychangers, and the seats of them that sold doves; and would not suffer that any man should carry any vessel through the temple. And he taught, saying,

My house is the house of prayer. Is it not written,
My house shall be called of all nations the house of
prayer? But ye have made it a den of thieves.

The scribes and chief priests heard it, and sought how they might destroy Jesus: for they feared him, because all the people were very attentive to hear him.

When even was come, he went out of the city.

In the morning, as they came by, they saw the fig tree dried up from the roots. And Peter, calling to remembrance, said to Jesus, Master, behold, the fig tree which thou cursed is withered away.

Jesus answered,

Have faith in God. For verily I say unto you that whosoever shall say unto this mountain, Be thou removed, and be thou cast into the sea; and shall not doubt in his heart, but shall believe that those things which he saith shall come to pass, he shall have whatsoever he saith.

Therefore I say unto you, what things soever ye desire, when ye pray, believe that ye receive them, and ye shall receive them.

And when ye stand praying, forgive, if ye have ought against any: that your Father also which is in heaven may forgive you your trespasses. But if ye do not forgive, neither will your Father which is in heaven forgive your trespasses.

Christ's authority is questioned

Matthew 21:23–46; Mark 11:27–33; 12:1–12; Luke 20, 1–19

On one of those days, as Jesus was walking in the temple and preaching the gospel, the chief priests and the scribes came with the elders, saying, By what authority doest thou these things

Jesus answered,

I also will ask of you one question, which if ye will answer me, I in likewise will tell you by what authority I do these things. The baptism of John, whence was it? Was it from heaven, or of men? Answer me.

They reasoned with themselves, saying, If we shall say, From heaven, he will say, Why then did ye not believe him? But if we shall say, Of men, the people will stone us: for they be persuaded that John was indeed a prophet.

They feared the people. And they answered, We cannot tell.

Jesus said to them,

Neither tell I you by what authority I do these things.

Then he began to speak in parables:

But what think ye? A certain man had two sons; and he came to the first, and said, Son, go and work today in my vineyard. He answered and said, I will not: but afterwards he repented, and went. And he came to the second, and said likewise. And he answered and said, I go, sir: and went not.

Whether of them twain did the will of his father?

They say, The first.
Jesus replied,

Verily I say unto you that the publicans and the harlots go into the kingdom of God before you. For John came unto you in the way of righteousness, and ye believed him not: but the publicans and the harlots believed him; and ye, when ye had seen it, repented not afterwards, that ye might believe him.

Hear another parable. There was a certain householder, which planted a vineyard, and set a hedge round about it, and dug a place in it for the winevat; and dug a winepress in it; and built a tower, and let it out to husbandmen, and went into a far country for a long time.

And at the season when the time of the fruit drew near, he sent a servant to the husbandmen, that he might receive from them of the fruit of the vineyard: but the husbandmen caught him, and beat him, and sent him away empty.

And again he sent unto them another servant; they beat him also, and at him they cast stones, and wounded him in the head, and handled him shamefully, and sent him away empty.

And again he sent a third: and him they wounded also, and killed, and they cast him out: and many others, more than the first: and they did unto them likewise, beating some, and killing some.

Then said the lord of the vineyard, What shall I do? I will send my beloved son. It may be they will reverence him when they see him.

But when those husbandmen saw the son, they reasoned among themselves, saying, This is the heir; come, let us kill him, and let us seize on his inheritance, and the inheritance shall be ours.

So they caught him, and slew him, and cast him out of the vineyard.

When the lord therefore of the vineyard cometh, what will he do unto those husbandmen? He will come and miserably destroy those wicked men, and

*will let out his vineyard unto other husbandmen,
which shall render him the fruits in their seasons.*

When they heard it, they said, God forbid.
Jesus beheld them, and said,

*Did ye never read in the scriptures? What is this
then that is written? The stone which the builders
rejected, the same is become the head of the corner:
this was the Lord's doing, and it is marvellous in
our eyes.*

*Therefore I say unto you, the kingdom of God
shall be taken from you, and given to a nation
bringing forth the fruits thereof. And whosoever
shall fall on this stone shall be broken: but on
whomsoever it shall fall, it will grind him to powder.*

The chief priests and Pharisees heard Jesus's parables and
perceived that he had spoken the parables against them. And

they sought to lay hold on him, but feared the people, because they took him for a prophet; so they left him, and went their way.

Jesus confounds the Pharisees and silences the Sadducees

Matthew 22:1–32; Mark 12:13–27; Luke 20:20–38

Jesus spoke to them again a parable,

The kingdom of heaven is like unto a certain king which made a marriage for his son, and sent forth his servants to call them that were bidden to the wedding: and they would not come.

Again, he sent forth other servants, saying, Tell them which are bidden, Behold, I have prepared my dinner: my oxen and my fatlings are killed, and all things are ready: come unto the marriage. But they made light of it, and went their ways, one to his farm, another to his merchandise; and the remnant took his servants, and entreated them spitefully, and slew them. And when the king heard thereof, he was wroth: and sent forth his armies, and destroyed those murderers, and burned up their city.

Then saith he to his servants, The wedding is ready, but they which were bidden were not worthy. Go ye therefore into the highways, and as many as ye shall find, bid to the marriage. So those servants went out into the highways, and gathered all together as many as they found, both bad and good: and the wedding was furnished with guests.

And when the king came in to see the guests, he saw there a man which had not on a wedding garment: and he saith unto him, Friend how camest thou in hither not having a wedding garment? And the man was speechless.

Then said the king to the servants, Bind him hand and foot, and take him away, and cast him *into outer darkness; there shall be weeping and gnashing of teeth.*

For many are called, but few are chosen.

Then the Pharisees took counsel how they might entangle Jesus in his talk. They sent spies to catch him in his words and deliver him to the authority of the governor.

When these were come, they said to Jesus, Master, we know that thou teachest the way of God in truth, neither acceptest the person of men. Tell us, Is it lawful to give tribute to Caesar, or not?

Jesus perceived their craftiness, and said.

Why tempt ye me, ye hypocrites? Show me the tribute money; bring me a penny, that I may see it. Show me a penny.

And they brought it.
He asked them,

Whose is this image and superscription?

They answered, Caesar's.

Then said he,

Render therefore unto Caesar the things which be Caesar's; and unto God the things which be God's.

They marvelled at his answers; they held their peace, and left him.

The same day came Sadducees, which say that there is no resurrection, and they asked Jesus, saying, Moses wrote, If a man die, and leave his wife behind him, and leave no children, his brother shall marry the wife and raise up seed unto his brother.

Now there were seven brethren: the first took a wife, and died without children; the second took her to wife and he died childless; the third likewise; and in like manner the seven also: they died, and left no children. Last of all, the woman died. Therefore in the resurrection whose wife of them is she?

Jesus answering said,

Ye do err, not knowing the scriptures, nor the power of God.

The children of this world marry, and are given

in marriage; but they which shall be accounted worthy to obtain that world, and the resurrection from the dead, when they shall rise from the dead, they neither marry, nor are given in marriage: for they are equal unto the angels of God which are in heaven; and are the children of God, being the children of the resurrection.

And as touching the resurrection of the dead, that they rise, have ye not read in the book of Moses that which was spoken unto you by God: how in the bush God spake unto Moses, saying, I am the God of Abraham, and the God of Isaac, and the God of Jacob?

God is not the God of the dead, but the God of the living; for all live unto him: ye therefore do greatly err.

The greatest of the commandments

Matthew 22:34–46; Mark 12:28–44; Luke 20:41–47; 21:1–4

The Pharisees had heard that Jesus had put the Sadducees to silence, and one of them which was a lawyer, perceiving that Jesus had answered the Sadducees well, asked him, tempting him, Master, which is the great commandment in the law? Which is the first commandment of all?

Jesus said unto him,

The first of all the commandments is, Hear, O Israel, The Lord our God is one Lord: and thou shalt love the Lord thy God with all thy heart, and with all thy soul, and with all thy mind, and with all thy strength: this is the first and great commandment. And the second is like unto it, namely this, Thou shalt love thy neighbour as thyself. On these two commandments hang all the law and the prophets. There is none other commandment greater than these.

And the scribe said, Well, Master, thou hast said the truth: for there is one God; and there is none other: and to love him with all the heart, and with all the understanding, and with all the soul, and with all the strength: and to love his neighbour as himself, is more than all burnt offerings and sacrifices.

Jesus saw that he answered discreetly; and said unto him,

Thou art not far from the kingdom of God.

While the Pharisees were gathered together, Jesus asked them,

What think ye of Christ? Whose son is he?

They say unto him, The son of David.
He saith unto them,

How then doth David in spirit call him Lord, saying, The Lord said unto my Lord, Sit thou on my right hand, till I make thine enemies thy

footstool? If David then call him Lord, how is he his son?

And no man was able to answer him a word: neither durst any man from that day forth ask him any more questions. The common people heard him gladly.

While Jesus taught in the temple, he said,

How say the scribes that Christ is David's son? For in the book of Psalms David himself saith, by the Holy Ghost, The Lord said unto my Lord, Sit thou on my right hand, till I make thine enemies thy footstool. David therefore himself calleth him Lord; and how is he then his son?

Then in the audience of all the people he said unto his disciples,

Beware of the scribes, which desire to walk in long robes, and love greetings in the marketplaces, and

the highest seats in the synagogues, and the uppermost rooms at feasts; which devour widows' houses, and for a show make long prayers: these same shall receive greater damnation.

Jesus sat over against the treasury. He beheld people cast money and gifts into the treasury. Many that were rich cast in much. He saw also a certain poor widow casting in thither two mites, which make a farthing.

He called his disciples, and saith unto them,

Of a truth, I say unto you that this poor widow doth cast in more than they all which have cast into the treasury: for all these have of their abundance cast in unto the offerings of God: but she of her penury did cast in all that she had, even all her living.

Jesus speaks out against hypocrisy

Matthew 23:1–39

To the multitude and to his disciples, Jesus spoke, saying,

The scribes and the Pharisees sit in Moses' seat: all therefore whatsoever they bid you observe, that observe and do; but do not ye after their works: for they say, and do not. For they bind heavy burdens and grievous to be borne, and lay them on men's shoulders; but they themselves will not move them with one of their fingers.

But all their works they do for to be seen of men: they make broad their phylacteries, and enlarge the borders of their garments, and love the uppermost rooms at feasts, and the chief seats in the synagogues, and greetings in the markets, and to be called of men, Rabbi, Rabbi. But be not ye called

Rabbi: for one is your Master, even Christ; and all ye are brethren.

And call no man your father upon the earth: for one is your Father which is in heaven. Neither be ye called masters: for one is your Master, even Christ.

But he that is greatest among you shall be your servant. And whosoever shall exalt himself shall be abased; and he that shall humble himself shall be exalted.

But woe unto you, scribes and pharisees, hypocrites! for ye shut up the kingdom of heaven against men: for ye neither go in yourselves, neither suffer ye them that are entering to go in.

Woe unto you, scribes and Pharisees, hypocrites! for ye devour widows' houses and for a pretence make long prayer; therefore ye shall receive the greater damnation.

Woe unto you, scribes and Pharisees, hypocrites! for ye compass sea and land to make one proselyte, and when he is made, ye make him twofold more the child of hell than yourselves.

Woe unto you, ye blind guides, which say whosoever shall swear by the temple, it is nothing; but whosoever shall swear by the gold of the temple, he is a debtor!

Ye fools and blind: for whether is greater, the gold or the temple that sanctifieth the gold?

And whosoever shall swear by the altar, it is nothing; but whosoever sweareth by the gift that is upon it, he is guilty.

Ye fools and blind; for whether is greater, the gift or the altar that sactifieth the gift?

Whoso therefore shall swear by the altar, sweareth by it, and by all things thereon.

And whoso shall swear by the temple, sweareth by it, and by him that dwelleth therein.

And he that shall swear by heaven, sweareth by the throne of God, and by him that sitteth thereon.

Woe unto you, scribes and Pharisees, hypocrites! for ye pay tithe of mint and anise and cummin, and have omitted the weightier matters of the law, judgment, mercy and faith: these ought ye to have done and not to leave the other undone.Ye blind guides, which strain at a gnat and swallow a camel.

Woe unto you, scribes and Pharisees, hypocrites! for ye make clean the outside of the cup and of the platter, but within they are full of extortion and excess. Thou blind Pharisee, cleanse first that which is within the cup and platter that the outside of them may be clean also.

Woe unto you, scribes and Pharisees, hypocrites!

for ye are like unto whited sepulchres, which indeed appear beautiful outward, but are within full of dead men's bones, and of all uncleanness. Even so ye also outwardly appear righteous unto men, but within ye are full of hypocrisy and iniquity.

Woe unto you, scribes and Pharisees, hypocrites! because ye build the tombs of the prophets and garnish the sepulchres of the righteous, and say, If we had been in the days of our fathers, we would not have been partakers with them in the blood of the prophets.

Wherefore ye be witnesses unto yourselves that ye are the children of them which killed the prophets. Fill ye up then the measure of your fathers. Ye serpents, ye generation of vipers, how can ye escape the damnation of hell?

Wherefore, behold, I send unto you prophets, and

wise men, and scribes: and some of them ye shall kill and crucify; and some of them shall ye scourge in your synagogues, and persecute them from city to city: that upon you may come all the righteous blood shed upon the earth, from the blood of righteous Abel unto the blood of Zacharias, son of Barachias, whom ye slew between the temple and the altar. Verily I say unto you, all these things shall come upon this generation.

O Jerusalem, Jerusalem, thou that killest the prophets, and stonest them which are sent unto thee, how often would I have gathered thy children together, even as a hen gathereth her chickens under her wings, and ye would not!

Behold, your house is left unto you desolate. For I say unto you, Ye shall not see me henceforth, till ye shall say, Blessed is he that cometh in the name of the Lord.

Jesus explains that the hour has come

John 12:20–36, 42–50

Certain Greeks came up to worship at the feast: the same came to Philip, saying, Sir, we would see Jesus.

Philip and Andrew told Jesus, who answered them, saying,

The hour is come that the Son of man should be glorified.

Verily, verily, I say unto you, except a corn of wheat fall into the ground and die, it abideth alone: but if it die it bringeth forth much fruit. He that loveth his life shall lose it; and he that hateth his life in his world shall keep it unto life eternal.

If any man serve me, let him follow me; and where I am, there shall also my servant be: if any man serve me, him will my Father honour.

*Now is my soul troubled; and what shall I say?
Father, save me from this hour? but for this cause
came I unto this hour.*

Father, glorify thy name.

Then came there a voice from heaven saying, I have both glorified it, and will glorify it again.

The people that stood by said that it thundered; others said, An angel spoke to him.

Jesus said,

*This voice came not because of me, but for your
sakes. Now is the judgment of this world: now shall
the prince of this world be cast out. And I, if I be
lifted up from the earth, will draw all men unto me.*

This he said, signifying what death he should die.

The people answered, We have heard out of the law that Christ abideth for ever; and how sayest thou, The Son of man must be lifted up? Who is this Son of man?

Then Jesus said,

Yet a little while is the light with you. Walk while ye have the light, lest darkness come upon you: for he that walketh in darkness knoweth not whither he goeth. While ye have light, believe in the light, that ye may be the children of light.

Among the chief rulers many believed on Jesus; but because of the Pharisees they did not confess him, lest they should be put out of the synagogue: for they loved the praise of men more than the praise of God.

Jesus cried and said,

He that believeth on me believeth not on me but on him that sent me. And he that seeth me seeth him that sent me.

I am come a light into the world, that whosoever believeth on me should not abide in darkness. And if any man hear my words, and believe not, I judge him not: for I came not to judge the world, but to save the world.

He that rejecteth me, and receiveth not my words, hath one that judgeth him: the word that I have spoken, the same shall judge him in the last day. For I have not spoken of myself; but the Father which sent me, he gave me a commandment, what I should say, and what I should speak. And I know that his commandment is life everlasting: whatsoever I speak therefore, even as the Father said unto me, so I speak.

Jesus foretells the destruction of the temple and the second coming

Matthew 24:1–31; Mark 13:1–27; Luke 21:5–28

As Jesus went out of the temple, his disciples came to show him the buildings of the temple. One said, Master, see what buildings are here! See how they are adorned with goodly stones and gifts.

Jesus answering said,

Seest thou these great buildings? See ye not all these things? Verily I say unto you, as for these things which ye behold, the days will come in the which there shall not be left here one stone upon another that shall not be thrown down.

As Jesus sat upon the Mount of Olives, over against the temple, Peter and James and John and Andrew asked him privately, What sign will there be when these things shall come to pass? What shall be the sign of thy coming, and of the end of the world?

Jesus replied,

Take heed lest any man deceive you. For many shall come in my name, saying, I am Christ, and shall deceive many; and the time draweth near; go ye not therefore after them.

Take heed that ye be not deceived, but when ye shall hear commotions, and wars, and rumours of wars, see that ye be not troubled; be not terrified. Such things must needs be; all these things must first come to pass; but the end shall not be yet.

Nation shall rise against nation, and kingdom against kingdom; and there shall be famines, and troubles, and pestilences, and great earthquakes, in divers places; and fearful sights and great signs shall there be from heaven. All these things are the beginnings of sorrows.

But take heed to yourselves: for before all these,

they shall lay their hands on you, and persecute you; delivering you up to councils, and into prisons, to be afflicted: and in the synagogues ye shall be beaten and ye shall be brought before rulers and kings for my name's sake. And it shall turn to you for a testimony against them. Then shall they kill you, and ye shall be hated of all nations for my name's sake.

But the gospel must first be published among all nations.

And when they shall lead you, and deliver you up, take no thought beforehand what ye shall speak, neither do ye premeditate: but whatsoever shall be given you in that hour, that speak ye, for it is not ye that speak, but the Holy Ghost. Settle it therefore in your hearts, not to meditate before what ye shall answer; for I will give you a mouth and wisdom, which all your adversaries shall not be able to gainsay nor resist.

And then shall many be offended, and shall betray one another. And ye shall be betrayed both by parents, and brethren, and kinsfolks, and friends. Now the brother shall betray the brother to death, and the father the son; and children shall rise up against their parents, and shall cause them to be put to death; and some of you shall they cause to be put to death. And ye shall be hated of all men for my name's sake.

But there shall not a hair of your head perish. In your patience possess ye your souls.

And many false prophets shall rise and shall deceive many. And because iniquity shall abound, the love of many shall wax cold. But he that shall endure unto the end, the same shall be saved. And this gospel of the kingdom shall be preached in all the world for a witness unto all nations; and then shall the end come.

When ye therefore shall see the abomination of desolation, spoken of by Daniel the prophet, standing in the holy place, where it ought not (let him that readeth understand): and when ye shall see Jerusalem compassed with armies, then know that the desolation thereof is nigh: then let them which are in Judea flee to the mountains: and let them which are in the midst of it depart out; and let not them that are in the countries enter thereinto. And let him that is on the housetop not come down into the house, neither enter therein to take anything out of his house; and let him which is in the field not return back to take his clothes. For these be the days of vengeance, that all things which are written may be fulfilled.

And woe unto them that are with child, and to them that give suck, in those days! for there shall be great distress in the land, and wrath upon the people. And pray ye that your flight be not in winter, neither on the sabbath day: for in those days shall be great affliction; tribulation such as was not since the beginning of the creation which God created unto this time; no, nor ever in the world shall be. And except that the Lord had shortened those days, there should no flesh be saved. But for the elect's sake, whom he hath chosen, those days shall be shortened.

And they shall fall by the edge of the sword, and shall be led away captive into all nations: and Jerusalem shall be trodden down of the Gentiles, until the times of the Gentiles be fulfilled.

And then if any man shall say to you, Lo, here is Christ; or, Lo, he is there; believe it not: for there shall arise false Christs and false prophets, and shall show great signs and wonders to seduce, if it were possible, even the elect.

But take ye heed: behold, I have foretold you all things. Wherefore if they shall say unto you, Behold, he is in the desert – go not forth; Behold, he is in the secret chambers – believe it not. For as the lightning cometh out of the east and shineth even unto the west, so shall also the coming of the Son of man be. For wheresoever the carcass is, there will the eagles be gathered together.

But immediately, in those days after that tribulation, there shall be signs in the sun, and in the moon, and in the stars: the sun shall be darkened, and the moon shall not give her light, and the stars of heaven shall fall; and the powers that are in the heavens shall be shaken; and upon the earth shall be distress of nations, with perplexity; the sea and waves roaring; men's hearts failing them for fear, and for looking after those things which are coming on the earth; for the powers of heaven shall be shaken.

And then shall appear the sign of the Son of man in heaven: and then shall all the tribes of the earth mourn, and they shall see the Son of man coming in the clouds of heaven with power and great glory.

And then shall he send his angels with a great sound of a trumpet, and they shall gather together his elect from the four winds, from the uttermost part of the earth to the uttermost part of heaven; from one end of heaven to the other.

And when these things begin to come to pass,

then look up and lift up your heads; for your redemption draweth nigh.

Watch and pray

Matthew 24:32–51; 25: 1–13; Mark 13:28–37; Luke 21:29–36

Now learn a parable of the fig tree and all the trees. When the branch is yet tender, and putteth forth leaves, ye know that summer is nigh.

So in like manner, when ye shall see all these things come to pass, know ye that the kingdom of God is at hand, even at the doors. Verily I say unto you, this generation shall not pass till all these things be done. Heaven and earth shall pass away, but my words shall not pass away.

And take heed to yourselves, lest at any time your hearts be overcharged with surfeiting, and drunkenness, and cares of this life, so that the day come upon you unawares. For as a snare shall it come on all them that dwell on the face of the whole earth.

Watch ye therefore, and pray always, that ye may be accounted worthy to escape all these things that shall come to pass, and to stand before the Son of man.

But of that day and that hour knoweth no man, no, not the angels which are in heaven, neither the Son, but my Father only.

Take ye heed, watch and pray: for ye know not when the time is. But as the days of Noe were, so shall also the coming of the Son of man be. For as in the days that were before the flood they were eating and drinking, marrying and giving in marriage, until the day that Noe entered into the ark, and knew not till the flood came, and took them all away: so shall also the coming of the Son *of man be. Then shall two be in the field; the one shall be taken and the other left. Two women shall be grinding at the mill; the one shall be taken and the other left. Watch therefore: for ye know not at what hour your Lord doth come.*

For the Son of man is as a man taking a far journey, who left his house, and gave authority to his servants, and to every man his work, and commanded the porter to watch.

Watch ye therefore: for ye know not when the master of the house cometh – at even, or at midnight, or at the cockcrowing, or in the morning: lest coming suddenly he find you sleeping.

But know this, that if the goodman of the house had known in what watch the thief would come, he would have watched, and would not have suffered his house to be broken up. Therefore be ye also ready: for in such an hour as ye think not, the Son of man cometh. And what I say unto you, I say unto all, Watch.

Who then is a faithful and wise servant, whom his lord hath made ruler over his household, to give them meat in due season?

Blessed is that servant, whom his lord when he cometh shall find so doing. Verily I say unto you that he shall make him ruler over all his goods.

But and if that evil servant shall say in his heart, My lord delayeth his coming; and shall begin to smite his fellow servants, and to eat and drink with the drunken; the lord of that servant shall come in a day when he looketh not for him, and in an hour that he is not aware of, and shall cut him asunder, and appoint him his portion with the hypocrites: there shall be weeping and gnashing of teeth.

Then shall the kingdom of heaven be likened unto ten virgins, which took their lamps, and went forth to meet the bridegroom. And five of them were wise, and five were foolish. They that were foolish took their lamps, and took no oil with them. But the wise took oil in their vessels with their lamps.

While the bridegroom tarried, they all slumbered and slept. And at midnight there was a cry made, Behold, the bridegroom cometh; go ye out to meet him.

Then all those virgins arose, and trimmed their lamps. And the foolish said unto the wise, Give us of your oil; for our lamps are gone out. But the wise answered, saying, Not so; lest there be not enough for us and you; but go ye rather to them that sell, and buy for yourselves.

And while they went to buy, the bridegroom came: and they that were ready went in with him to the marriage: and the door was shut.

Afterward came also the other virgins, saying, Lord, Lord, open to us. But he answered and said, Verily I say unto you, I know you not.

Watch, therefore, for ye know neither the day nor the hour wherein the Son of man cometh.

The parable of the talents

Matthew 25:14–46

For the kingdom of heaven is as a man travelling into a far country, who called his own servants and delivered unto them his goods. And unto one he gave five talents, to another, two, and to another, one; to every man according to his several ability; and straightway took his journey.

Then he that had received the five talents went and traded with the same, and made another five talents. And likewise he that had received two, he gained another two. But he that had received one went and dug in the earth, and hid his lord's money.

After a long time the lord of those servants cometh, and reckoned with them.

And so he that had received five talents came and brought the other five talents, saying, Lord, thou deliveredst unto me five talents: behold, I have gained beside them five talents more. His lord said unto him, Well done, thou good and faithful servant: thou hast been faithful over a few things, I will make thee ruler over many things: enter thou into the joy of thy lord.

He also that had received two talents came and said, Lord, thou deliveredst unto me two talents: behold, I have gained two other talents beside them. His lord said unto him, Well done, good and faithful servant: thou hast been faithful over a few things, I will make thee ruler over many things: enter thou into the joy of thy lord.

Then he which had received the one talent came and said, Lord, I knew thee that thou art a hard man, reaping where thou hast not sown, and gathering where thou hast not strewed; and I was afraid, and went and hid thy talent in the earth: lo, there thou hast that is thine.

His lord answered and said unto him, Thou wicked and slothful servant, thou knewest that I reap where I sowed not, and gather where I have not strewed. Thou oughtest therefore to have put my money to the exchangers, and then at my coming I should have received mine own with usury.

Take therefore the talent from him, and give it unto him which hath ten talents.

For unto every one that hath shall be given, and he shall have abundance: but from him that hath not shall be taken away even that which he hath. And cast ye the unprofitable servant into outer darkness: there shall be weeping and gnashing of teeth.

When the Son of man shall come in his glory, and all the holy angels with him, then shall he sit upon the throne of his glory: and before him shall be gathered all nations: and he shall separate them one from another, as a shepherd divideth his sheep from the goats: and he shall set the sheep on his right hand, but the goats on the left.

Then shall the King say unto them on his right hand, Come, ye blessed of my Father, inherit the kingdom prepared for you from the foundation of the world: for I was hungry, and ye gave me meat; I was thirsty, and ye gave me drink; I was a stranger, and ye took me in; naked, and ye clothed me; I was sick, and ye visited me; I was in prison, and ye came unto me.

Then shall the righteous answer him, saying, Lord, when saw we thee hungry, and fed thee? or thirsty, and gave thee drink? When saw we thee a stranger, and took thee in? or naked, and clothed thee? Or when saw we thee sick, or in prison, and came unto thee?

And the King shall answer and say unto them, Verily I say unto you, inasmuch as ye have done it unto one of the least of these my brethren, ye have done it unto me.

Then shall he say also unto them on the left hand, Depart from me, ye cursed, into everlasting fire prepared for the devil and his angels: for I was hungry, and ye gave me no meat; I was thirsty, and ye gave me no drink; I was a stranger, and ye took me not in; naked, and ye clothed me not; sick, and in prison, and ye visited me not.

Then shall they also answer him, saying, Lord, when saw we thee hungry, or thirsty, or a stranger, or naked, or sick, or in prison, and did not minister unto thee?

Then he shall answer them, saying, Verily I say unto you, inasmuch as ye did it not to one of the least of these, ye did it not to me.

And these shall go away into everlasting punishment: but the righteous into life eternal.

The alabaster box of ointment

John 12:1–11; Matthew 26:6–13; Mark 14:3–9

Six days before the Passover, Jesus came to Bethany, where Lazarus was, whom he had raised from the dead. In the house of Simon the leper, they made Jesus a supper, and Martha served. Lazarus was one of them at the table with Jesus.

Mary, having an alabaster box of spikenard ointment, very precious, broke the box, and poured it on Jesus's head as he sat at meat, and anointed his feet, and wiped his feet with her hair.

Some disciples demanded indignantly, To what purpose is this waste? Judas Iscariot (which should betray Jesus) saith, Why was not this ointment sold for three hundred pence, and given to the poor? And they murmured against Mary.

When Jesus understood it, he said.

Let her alone: why trouble ye the woman? Against the day of my burying hath she done this.

For ye have the poor with you always, and whensoever ye will ye may do them good: but me ye have not always. She hath wrought a good work upon me; for she hath done what she could: for in that she hath poured this ointment on my body, she is come aforehand to anoint my body to the burying. Why trouble ye her?

Verily I say unto you, wheresoever this gospel shall be preached throughout the whole world, this that this woman hath done shall be told for a memorial of her.

The Jews knew that Jesus was there: and they came, not for Jesus's sake only, but that they might see Lazarus, whom he had raised from the dead.

But the chief priests consulted that they might put Lazarus also to death; because many of the Jews believed on Jesus because of him.

His betrayal imminent, Jesus washes the feet of the disciples

Luke 21:37–38; 22: 1–18; Matthew 26, 1–5, 14–20; Mark 14, 1–2, 10–17; John 13, 2–17

Now the feast of unleavened bread drew nigh. In the daytime Jesus was teaching in the temple. At night he abode in the Mount of Olives; in the morning the people came early to the temple to hear him.

Two days before the Passover, the chief priests, the scribes, and the elders of the people, assembled unto the palace of the high priest Caiaphas, and consulted how they might take Jesus by craft. But they said, Not on the feast day, lest there be an uproar of the people.

Then Judas surnamed Iscariot, one of the twelve, went and said unto the chief priests, What will ye give me if I deliver Jesus unto you? They were glad and convenanted to give Judas thirty pieces of silver. Judas agreed and sought an opportunity to betray Jesus to them in the absence of the multitude.

Now before the feast of the Passover, when Jesus knew that his hour was come, he said to his disciples,

Ye know that after two days is the feast of Passover, and the Son of man is betrayed to be crucified.

And on the first day of the feast, when the passover must be killed, Jesus sent Peter and John, saying,

Go and prepare the passover, that we may eat.

And they said, Where wilt thou that we prepare?
He said,

When ye are entered into the city, behold, there shall meet you a man bearing a pitcher of water; go ye into the city to such a man, and follow him into the house where he entereth in. And wheresoever he shall go in, say ye to the goodman of the house, The Master saith unto thee, My time is at hand; I will keep the Passover at thy house with my disciples. Where is the guest chamber where I shall eat the passover with my disciples?

And he will show you a large upper room furnished and prepared: there make ready for us.

They went, and found as he had said, and in the evening Jesus came there with the twelve apostles.

And he said to them.

With desire I have desired to eat this passover with you before I suffer: for I say unto you, I will not any more eat thereof, until it be fulfilled in the kingdom of God.

And he took the cup, and gave thanks, and said,

Take this, and divide it among yourselves: for I say unto you, I will not drink of the fruit of the vine, until the kingdom of God shall come.

Later, when supper was ended, Jesus laid aside his garments, and took a towel, and girded himself. Then he poured water into a basin, and began to wash the disciples' feet, and to wipe them with the towel.

Simon Peter said, Lord, dost thou wash my feet?
Jesus answered,

What I do thou knowest not now; but thou shalt know hereafter.

Peter said, Thou shalt never wash my feet.
Jesus answered.

If I wash thee not, thou hast no part with me.

Peter said, Lord, not my feet only, but also my hands and my head.
Jesus told him,

He that is washed needeth not save to wash his feet but is clean every whit: and ye are clean, but not all.

For he knew who should betray him; therefore he said,

Ye are not all clean.

So after he had washed their feet and had taken his garments, and was set down again, he said unto them,

Know ye what I have done to you?

Ye call me Master and Lord: and ye say well; for so I am. If I then, your Lord and Master, have washed your feet, ye also ought to wash one another's feet. For I have given you an example that ye should do as I have done to you.

Verily, verily, I say unto you, the servant is not greater than his lord: neither is he that is sent greater than he that sent him. If ye know these things, happy are ye if ye do them.

Jesus institutes his holy supper

I Corinthians 11:24–25; Matthew 26:21–29; Mark 14:18–25; Luke 22:19–38; John 13:18–38; 14, 1–4

The same night in which he was betrayed, the Lord Jesus took bread, and gave thanks, and blessed it, and brake it, and gave it to his disciples, and said,

Take, eat; this is my body, which is given for you: this do in remembrance of me.

As they sat and did eat, Jesus said,

Verily I say unto you that one of you shall betray me. But, behold, the hand of him that betrayeth me is with me on the table. And truly the Son of man goeth, as it was determined; but woe unto that man by whom he is betrayed!

I speak not of you all: I know whom I have chosen: but that the scripture may be fulfilled, he

that eateth bread with me hath lifted up his heel against me.

Now I tell you before it come, that when it is come to pass ye may believe that I am he.

Verily, verily, I say unto you, he that receiveth whomsoever I send receiveth me; and he that receiveth me receiveth him that sent me.

When Jesus had thus said, he was troubled in spirit; and he repeated,

Verily, verily, I say unto you, that one of you which eateth with me shall betray me.

The disciples looked one on another, doubting of whom he spoke. They were exceeding sorrowful, and began to say unto Jesus, one by one, Lord, is it I? and another, Is it I?

He answered,

It is one of the twelve that dippeth with me in the dish: the same shall betray me.

The Son of man indeed goeth, as it is written of him; but woe to that man by whom the Son of man is betrayed! Good were it for that man if he had never been born.

Now there was leaning on Jesus's bosom one whom Jesus loved. Simon Peter signalled to him that he should ask who it was of whom Jesus spoke.

And he asked, Lord, who is it?

Jesus answered,

He it is to whom I shall give a sop when I have dipped it.

He dipped the sop and gave it to Judas Iscariot and said,

That thou doest, do quickly.

Judas said Master, Is it I?

Jesus said unto him,

Thou hast said.

Judas went immediately out: and it was night.
When he was gone, Jesus said,

Now is the Son of man glorified, and God is glorified in him. If God be glorified in him, God shall also glorify him in himself, and shall straightway glorify him.

Little children, yet a little while I am with you. Ye shall seek me: and as I said unto the Jews, so now I say to you, whither I go, ye cannot come.

A new commandment I give unto you, that ye love one another; as I have loved you, so ye also love one another. By this shall all men know that ye are my disciples, if ye have love one for another.

Simon Peter said unto him, Lord, whither goest thou?
Jesus answered,

Whither I go, thou canst not follow me now: but thou shalt follow me afterwards.

Peter said, Lord, why cannot I follow thee now? I will lay down my life for thy sake.

Jesus answered,

Wilt thou lay down thy life for my sake? Verily, verily, I say unto thee, the cock shall not crow, till thou hast denied me thrice.

There was a strife among the disciples, which of them should be accounted the greatest. And Jesus said unto them,

The kings of the Gentiles exercise lordship over them; and they that exercise authority upon them are called benefactors. But ye shall not be so; but he that is greatest among you, let him be as the younger; and he that is chief, as he that doth serve.

For whether is greater, he that sitteth at meat, or he that serveth? Is it not he that sitteth at meat? But I am among you as he that serveth.

Ye are they which have continued with me in my temptations. And I appoint unto you a kingdom, as my father hath appointed unto me; that ye may eat and drink at my table in my kingdom, and sit on thrones judging the twelve tribes of Israel.

And the Lord said,

Simon, Simon, behold, Satan hath desired to have you, that he may sift you as wheat: but I have prayed for thee, that thy faith fail not: and when thou art converted, strengthen thy brethren.

And Simon said, Lord, I am ready to go with thee, both into prison and to death.

And Jesus said,

I tell thee, Peter, the cock shall not crow this day before thou shalt thrice deny that thou knowest me.

And he said unto them,

When I sent you without purse, and scrip, and shoes, lacked ye anything?

They said, Nothing.
Then said Jesus,

But now, he that hath a purse, let him take it, and likewise his scrip; and he that hath no sword, let him sell his garment, and buy one.

For I say unto you that this that is written must yet be accomplished in me: And he was reckoned among the transgressors.

For the things concerning me have an end.

And they said, Lord, behold, here are two swords.
And he answered,

It is enough.

When he had supped, Jesus took the cup, and when he had given thanks, gave it to them, saying,

Drink ye all of it.

And they all drank of it. And he said unto them,

This cup is the new testament in my blood, which is shed for you; this is my blood of the new testament which is shed for many for the remission of sins: this do ye, as oft as ye drink it, in remembrance of me.

Verily I say unto you, I will drink henceforth no more of the fruit of the vine, until that day when I drink it new with you in the kingdom of God, my Father's kingdom.

Let not your heart be troubled: ye believe in God, believe also in me. In my Father's house are many mansions: if it were not so, I would have told you. I

go to prepare a place for you. And if I go and prepare a place for you, I will come again, and receive you unto myself; that where I am, there ye may be also. And whither I go ye know, and the way ye know.

Jesus reassures the apostles

John 14:5–31

Thomas said to Jesus, Lord, we know not whither thou goest; and how can we know the way?

Jesus replied,

I am the way, the truth, and the life: no man cometh unto the Father, but by me. If ye had known me, ye should have known my Father also: and from henceforth ye know him, and have seen him.

Philip saith, Lord, show us the Father, and it sufficeth us. Jesus answered,

Have I been so long time with you, and yet hast thou not known me, Philip? He that hath seen me, hath seen the Father; and how sayest thou then, Show us the Father?

Believest thou not that I am in the Father, and the Father is in me? The words I speak unto you, I speak not of myself: but the Father that dwelleth in me, he doeth the works. Believe me that I am in the Father, and the Father is in me: or else believe me for the very works' sake.

Verily, verily, I say unto you, he that believeth on me, the works that I do shall he do also; and greater works than these shall he do; because I go unto my Father. And whatsoever ye shall ask in my name, that will I do, that the Father may be glorified in the Son. If ye shall ask anything in my name, I will do it.

If ye love me keep my commandments. And I will pray the Father, and he shall give you another Comforter, that he may abide with you for ever; even the Spirit of truth; whom the world cannot receive, because it seeth him not, neither knoweth him: but ye know him; for he dwelleth with you, and shall be in you. I will not leave you comfortless; I will come to you.

Yet a little while, and the world seeth me no more; but ye see me; because I live, ye shall live also. At that day ye shall know that I am in my Father, and ye in me, and I in you.

He that hath my commandments, and keepeth them, he it is that loveth me: and he that loveth me shall be loved of my Father, and I will love him, and will manifest myself to him.

Judas (not Iscariot) asked him, Lord, how is it that thou wilt manifest thyself unto us, and not unto the world?

Jesus answered,

If a man love me, he will keep my words: and my

Father will love him, and we will come unto him, and make our abode with him. He that loveth me not, keepeth not my sayings: and the word which ye hear is not mine, but the Father's which sent me.

These things have I spoken unto you, being yet present with you.

But the Comforter, which is the Holy Ghost, whom the Father will send in my name, he shall teach you all things, and bring all things to your remembrance, whatsoever I have said unto you. Peace I leave with you, my peace I give unto you: not as the world giveth, give I unto you.

Let not your heart be troubled, neither let it be afraid. Ye have heard how I said unto you, I go away, and come again unto you. If ye loved me, ye would rejoice, because I said, I go unto the Father: for my Father is greater than I.

And now I have told you, before it come to pass, that when it is come to pass, ye might believe.

Hereafter I will not talk much with you: for the prince of this world cometh, and hath nothing in me. But that the world may know that I love the Father; and as the Father gave me commandment, even so I do. Arise, let us go hence.

I am the true vine

John 15:1–27: 16:1

I am the true vine, and my Father is the husbandman. Every branch in me that beareth not fruit he taketh away: and every branch that beareth fruit, he purgeth it, that it may bring forth more fruit. Now ye are clean through the word which I have spoken unto you.

Abide in me, and I in you. As the branch cannot bear fruit of itself, except it abide in the vine, no more can ye, except ye abide in me. I am the vine, ye are the branches; he that abideth in me, and I in him, the same bringeth forth much fruit; for without me ye can do nothing.

If a man abide not in me, he is cast forth as a branch, and is withered; and men gather them, and cast them into the fire, and they are burned. If ye abide in me, and my words abide in you, ye shall ask what ye will, and it shall be done unto you.

Herein is my Father glorified, that ye bear much fruit; so shall ye be my disciples.

As the Father hath loved me, so have I loved you: continue ye in my love. If ye keep my commandments, ye shall abide in my love; even as I have kept my Father's commandments and abide in his love.

These things have I spoken unto you, that my joy might remain in you, and that your joy might be full. This is my commandment, that ye love one another as I have loved you.

Greater love hath no man than this, that a man lay down his life for his friends. Ye are my friends, if ye do whatsoever I command you. Henceforth I call *you not servants; for the servant knoweth not what his lord doeth; but I have called you friends; for all things that I have heard of my Father I have made known unto you.*

Ye have not chosen me, but I have chosen you, and ordained you, that ye should go and bring forth fruit, and that your fruit should remain: that whatsoever ye shall ask of the Father in my name, he may give it you. These things I command you, that ye love one another.

If the world hate you, ye know that it hated me before it hated you. If ye were of the world, the world would love his own: but because ye are not of the world, but I have chosen you out of the world, therefore the world hateth you.

Remember the word that I said unto you, the servant is not greater than his lord.

If they have persecuted me, they will also persecute you; if they have kept my saying, they will keep yours also. But all these things will they do unto you for my name's sake, because they know not him that sent me.

If I had not come and spoken unto them, they had not had sin: but now they have no cloak for their sin. He that hateth me hateth my Father also.

If I had not done among them the works which no other man did, they had not had sin: but now have they both seen and hated both me and my Father.

But this cometh to pass that the word might be fulfilled that is written in their law, They hated me without a cause.

But when the Comforter is come, whom I will send unto you from the Father, even the Spirit of truth, which proceedeth from the Father, he shall testify of me; and ye also shall bear witness, because ye have been with me from the beginning.

These things have I spoken unto you, that ye should not be offended.

Be of good cheer

John 16:2–33

They shall put you out of the synagogues: yea, the time cometh that whosoever killeth you will think that he doeth God's service. And these things will they do unto you, because they have not known the Father, nor me.

But these things have I told you that, when the time shall come, ye may remember that I told you of them. And these things I said not unto you at the beginning, because I was with you.

But now I go my way to him that sent me; and none of you asketh me, Whither goest thou? But because I have said these things unto you, sorrow hath filled your heart. Nevertheless, I tell you the truth. It is expedient for you that I go away: for if I go not away, the Comforter will not come unto you; but if I depart, 1 will send him unto you. And when he is come, he will reprove the world of sin, and of righteousness, and of judgment: of sin, because they believed not on me; of righteousness, because I go to my Father, and ye see me no more; of judgment, because the prince of this world is judged.

I have yet many things to say unto you, but ye cannot bear them now. Howbeit, when he, the Spirit of truth, is come, he will guide you into all truth: for he shall not speak of himself; but whatsoever he shall hear, that shall he speak: and he will show you things to come. He shall glorify me: for he shall receive of mine, and shall show it unto you.

*All things that the Father hath are mine:
therefore said I that he shall take of mine, and shall
show it unto you.*

*A little while, and ye shall not see me: and again,
a little while, and ye shall see me, because I go to
the Father.*

Then said some of his disciples among themselves, What is
this that he saith?

Now Jesus knew that they were desirous to ask him, and he
said,

*Do ye enquire among yourselves of that I said, A
little while, and ye shall not see me: and again, a
little while, and ye shall see me?*

*Verily, verily, I say unto you that ye shall weep
and lament, but the world shall rejoice; and ye
shall be sorrowful, but your sorrow shall be turned
into joy.*

A woman when she is in travail hath sorrow, because her hour is come: but as soon as she is delivered of the child, she remembereth no more the anguish for joy that a man is born into the world. And ye now therefore have sorrow: but I will see you again, and your heart shall rejoice, and your joy no man taketh from you.

And in that day ye shall ask me nothing. Verily, verily, I say unto you, whatsoever ye shall ask the Father in my name, he will give you. Hitherto have ye asked nothing in my name: ask, and ye shall receive, that your joy may be full.

These things have I spoken unto you in proverbs: but the time cometh when I shall no more speak unto you in proverbs, but I shall show you plainly of the Father. At that day ye shall ask in my name: and I say not unto you that I will pray the Father for you: for the Father himself loveth you, because ye have loved me, and have believed that I came out from God.

I came forth from the Father, and am come into the world; again, I leave the world, and go to the Father.

His disciples said unto him, Lo, now speakest thou plainly. Now we believe that thou camest forth from God.

Jesus answered,

Do ye now believe? Behold, the hour cometh, yea, is now come, that ye shall be scattered, every man to his own, and shall leave me alone; and yet I am not alone, because the Father is with me.

These things I have spoken unto you that in me ye might have peace. In the world ye shall have tribulation: but be of good cheer; I have overcome the world.

Christ prays

John 17:1–26

Jesus spoke these words and lifted up his eyes to heaven,

Father, the hour is come; glorify thy Son, that thy Son also may glorify thee: as thou hast given him power over all flesh, that he should give eternal life to as many as thou hast given him. And this is life eternal, that they might know thee the only true God, and Jesus Christ whom thou hast sent. I have glorified thee on the earth: I have finished the work which thou gavest me to do. And now, O Father, glorify thou me with thine own self with the glory which I had with thee before the world was.

I have manifested thy name unto the men which thou gavest me out of the world: thine they were, and thou gavest them me; and they have kept thy word. Now they have known that all things whatsoever thou hast given me are of thee. For I have given unto them the words which thou gavest me; and they have received them, and have known surely that I came out from thee, and they have believed that thou didst send me.

I pray for them: I pray not for the world, but for them which thou hast given me; for they are thine. And all mine are thine, and thine are mine; and I am glorified in them. And now I am no more in the world, but these are in the world, and I come to thee. Holy Father, keep through thine own name those whom thou hast given me, that they may be one, as we are. While I was with them in the world, I kept them in thy name: those that thou gavest me I have kept, and none of them is lost, but the son of perdition: that the scripture might be fulfilled.

And now come I to thee; and these things I speak in the world that they might have my joy fulfilled in themselves. I have given them thy word; and the world hath hated them, because they are not of the world, even as I am not of the world. I pray not that thou shouldest take them out of the world, but that thou shouldest keep them from the evil. They are not of the world, even as I am not of the world. Sanctify them through thy truth: thy word is truth. As thou hast sent me into the world, even so have I also sent them into the world. And for their sakes I sanctify myself that they also might be sanctified through the truth.

Neither pray I for these alone, but for them also which shall believe on me through their word; that they all may be one; as thou, Father, art in me, and I in thee, that they also may be one in us: that the world may believe that thou hast sent me. And the glory which thou gavest me I have given them: that they may be one, even as we are one; I in them, and thou in me, that they may be made perfect in one; and that the world may know that thou hast sent me, and hast loved them, as thou hast loved me.

Father, I will that they also, whom thou hast given me, be with me where I am; that they may behold my glory, which thou hast given me: for thou lovedst me before the foundation of the world.

O righteous Father, the world hath not known thee: but I have known thee, and these have known that thou hast sent me. And I have declared unto them thy name, and will declare it: that the love wherewith thou hast loved me may be in them, and I in them.

Arise, let us go hence.

The agony in the garden

Matthew 26:30–47; Mark 14:26–43; Luke 22:39–47; John 18:1–9

When they had sung a hymn, Jesus went to the Mount of Olives; and his disciples followed him. Then saith Jesus unto them,

All ye shall be offended, because of me this night: for it is written, I will smite the shepherd, and the sheep of the flock shall be scattered abroad.

But after that I am risen again, I will go before you into Galilee.

Peter answered, I will never be offended.
Jesus said to him,

Verily I say unto thee that this day, even in this night, before the cock crow twice, thou shalt deny me thrice.

But Peter spake the more vehemently, Though I should die with thee, yet will I not deny thee in any wise. Likewise said they all.

They came to a place named Gethsemane, over the brook Cedron, where was a garden. And he said unto them,

Sit ye here, while I go and pray yonder. Pray that ye enter not into temptation.

He was withdrawn from them about a stone's cast; with him were Peter, James and John. He said to them,

My soul is exceeding sorrowful, even unto death: tarry ye here, and watch with me.

He went forward a little, and kneeled, and prayed,

Abba, Father, all things are possible unto thee: Father, if it be possible, if thou be willing, remove this cup from me: nevertheless, not my will, but thine, be done.

Being in an agony he prayed more earnestly: and his sweat was as it were great drops of blood.

And he cometh unto the disciples, and findeth them sleeping. He said to Peter,

Simon, sleepest thou? What, couldest not thou watch with me one hour? Watch ye and pray, lest ye enter into temptation. The spirit truly is willing, but the flesh is weak.

Jesus went away the second time, and prayed,

O my Father, if it be possible, let this cup pass from me: if this cup may not pass away from me, except I drink it, thy will be done.

When he rose up, and was come again to the disciples, he found them sleeping for sorrow, and he said to them,

Why sleep ye? Rise and pray, lest ye enter into temptation.

He went and prayed the third time, saying the same words,

Father, take away this cup from me: nevertheless, not what I will, but what thou wilt.

And he cometh the third time, and again he found the disciples asleep; and he said,

Sleep on now, and take your rest: it is enough: behold, the hour is come; behold, the hour is at hand, and the Son of man is betrayed into the hands of sinners. Rise up, let us be going: lo, he is at hand that doth betray me.

Immediately, while Jesus yet spake, cometh Judas, and with him a multitude: a band of men from the chief priests and Pharisees; and the scribes and elders of the people, with lanterns and torches, and swords and staves.

Jesus went forth, and said to them,

Whom seek ye?

They answered, Jesus of Nazareth.

Jesus said,

I am he.

They stepped backwards, and fell to the ground.
Then asked he them again,

Whom seek ye?

They said, Jesus of Nazareth.
Jesus answered,

I have told you that I am he; if therefore ye seek me,
let these go their way.

Thus would be fulfilled the saying which he had spoken,

Of them which thou gavest me have I lost none.

Judas's kiss

Matthew 26:48–58; Mark 14:44–50, 53–54; Luke 22:47–55;
John 18:10–16, 19–23

Now Judas had said, Whomsoever I shall kiss, that same is he: hold him fast. Accordingly, he went before, and drew near unto Jesus to kiss him: and said, Hail, Master; and kissed him.

Jesus said to Judas,

Friend, wherefore art thou come? Judas, betrayest thou the Son of man with a kiss?

Then they laid hands on Jesus. They which were about him said, Lord, shall we smite them with the sword? And Peter, having a sword, smote the high priest's servant, Malchas, and cut off his right ear.

Jesus said,

Suffer thus far.

And he touched his ear and healed him. Then said Jesus unto Peter,

Put up again thy sword into its place in the sheath: for all they that take the sword shall perish with the sword. The cup which my Father hath given me, shall I not drink it? Thinkest thou that I cannot now pray to my Father, and he shall presently give me more than twelve legions of angels? But how then shall the scriptures be fulfilled, that thus it must be?

In that same hour said Jesus unto the multitude,

Be ye come out, as against a thief, with swords and staves for to take me? When I sat daily with you, teaching in the temple, ye stretched forth no hands against me: ye laid no hold on me: ye took me not: but this is your hour, and the power of darkness. But all this was done that the scriptures of the prophets might be fulfilled.

Then all the disciples forsook him, and fled.

The officers of the Jews bound Jesus and led him away. They brought him into the palace of the high priest, Caiaphas that year. Simon Peter followed, to see the end. And so did another disciple, who was known to Caiaphas and went with Jesus into the palace. But Peter stood at the door without. Then went out that disciple and spoke to her that kept the door and brought in Peter.

When they had kindled a fire in the midst of the hall, Peter sat amongst the servants, and warmed himself at the fire.

With Caiaphas were assembled the chief priests and the elders and the scribes. Caiaphas asked Jesus of his doctrine.

Jesus answered,

I spake openly to the world: I ever taught in the synagogues, and in the temple, whither the Jews always resort: and in secret have I said nothing. Ask them which heard me, what I have said unto them: behold, they know what I said. Why askest thou me?

When Jesus had thus spoken, one of the officers struck him with the palm of his hand, saying, Answerest thou the high priest so?

Jesus answered,

If I have spoken evil, bear witness to the evil: but if well, why smitest thou me?

Christ's trial

Matthew 26:59–75; 27:1–7; Mark 14:55–72; Luke 22:56–71;
John 18:17–27

The chief priests and all the council sought witness against
Jesus, to put him to death. Many bore false witness against him,
but their witness agreed not together.

The high priest arose, and asked Jesus, Answerest thou
nothing?

But Jesus held his peace.

The high priest said, Tell us whether thou be the Christ, the
Son of God.

And Jesus said,

*Thou hast said. I am. Nevertheless, I say unto you,
hereafter shall ye see the Son of man sitting on the
right hand of power, and coming in the clouds of
heaven.*

Then saith the high priest, Now ye have heard his blasphemy:
what need ye any further witnesses? What think ye?

They answered, He is guilty and must be put to death.

When they had blindfolded Jesus, they struck him on the face, and said unto him, Prophesy, who is it that smote thee?

*

Now Peter was beneath in the palace: and the damsel that kept the door came and looked upon him as he sat by the fire, and said, Thou also wast with Jesus of Galilee.

But he denied before them all, saying, I know him not: I know not, neither understand I what thou sayest.

And he went into the porch, and the cock crew.

After a little while another saw Peter, and said, Thou art also of them, for thou art a Galilean: thy speech betrayeth thee.

And Peter denied again, Man, I am not.

About the space of an hour after, another confidently affirmed, Of a truth this fellow was with Jesus.

But Peter began to swear, saying, I know not this man of whom ye speak.

And the second time the cock crew. Then Peter called to mind the words that Jesus said unto him,

Before the cock crow twice, thou shalt deny me thrice.

And when Peter thought thereon, he wept.

*

As soon as it was day, the elders of the people and the chief priests and the scribes led Jesus into their council, saying, Art thou the Christ?

And he said,

If I tell you, ye will not believe: and if I also ask you, ye will not answer me, nor let me go. Hereafter shall the Son of man sit on the right hand of the power of God.

Then said they, Art thou then the Son of God?
And Jesus said,

Ye say that I am.

They said, What need we any further witness? We ourselves have heard of his own mouth. And the whole council held a consultation, to put Jesus to death.

Judas, when he saw that Jesus was condemned, repented and

brought the thirty pieces of silver to the chief priests, saying, I have sinned in that I have betrayed the innocent blood.

They said, What is that to us? See thou to that.

Then Judas cast down the pieces of silver in the temple, and went and hanged himself.

The chief priests took the silver pieces and said, It is the price of blood: it is not lawful to put them into the treasury. They took counsel, and bought with them the potter's field, to bury strangers in.

Christ is brought before Pilate

John 18:28–40; 19:1–16; Luke 23:1–11, 13–25; Mark 15:1–15;
Matthew 27:11–26

The whole council arose and led Jesus away from the high priest,
Caiaphas, and delivered him to Pontius Pilate the governor, in
the hall of judgment.

Pilate went out to them, and said, Take ye him, and judge him
according to your law.

The Jews answered, It is not lawful for us to put any man to
death.

Then Pilate entered into the judgment hall again, and called
Jesus, and said unto him, Art thou the King of Jews?

Jesus answered,

*Sayest thou this thing of thyself, or did others tell it
thee of me?*

Pilate answered, Am I a Jew? Thine own nation have delivered
thee unto me: what hast thou done?

Jesus answered,

My kingdom is not of this world: if my kingdom were of this world, then would my servants fight that I should not be delivered to the Jews: but now is my kingdom not from hence.

Pilate therefore said, Art thou a king then?
Jesus answered,

Thou sayest that I am a king. To this end was I born, and for this cause came I into the world, that I should bear witness unto the truth. Every one that is of the truth heareth my voice.

Pilate answered, What is truth? And he went out again and said to the Jews, I find in him no fault at all. But ye have a custom that I should release unto you one at the Passover: will ye that I release the King of the Jews?

Then cried they all, Not this man, but Barabbas.

Now Barabbas was a robber, who for sedition and murder was cast into prison.

The chief priests and the officers cried out, Crucify him, crucify him.

Pilate saith, Take ye him, and crucify him: for I find no fault in him.

The Jews answered, By our law he ought to die, because he made himself the Son of God.

When Pilate heard that saying, he asked Jesus, Whence art thou? But Jesus gave no answer. Then Pilate said, Speakest thou not unto me? Knowest thou not that I have power to crucify thee, or to release thee?

Jesus answered,

Thou couldest have no power at all against me, except it were given thee from above: therefore he that delivered me unto thee hath the greater sin.

Thenceforth Pilate sought to release Jesus: but the Jews cried out, We found this fellow forbidding to give tribute to Caesar, saying that he himself is Christ the king. If thou let this man go, thou art not Caesar's friend: whosoever maketh himself a king speaketh against Caesar.

Pilate asked him. Art thou the King of the Jews?
And Jesus said,

Thou sayest it.

The chief priests accused him of many things: but he answered nothing.

And Pilate asked him again, Answerest thou nothing? Hearest thou not how many things they witness against thee?

Jesus answered him never a word; so that Pilate marvelled: and he said to the people, I find no fault in this man.

They were the more fierce, saying, He stirreth up the people throughout Jewry, from Galilee to this place.

When Pilate heard of Galilee, he asked whether the man were a Galilean. And as soon as he knew that Jesus belonged unto Herod's jurisdiction, he sent him to Herod, who was at Jerusalem at that time.

Herod was exceeding glad: for he had heard many things of Jesus and had hoped to see some miracle done by him. He questioned with Jesus in many words; but Jesus answered him nothing. And Herod sent him back to Pilate.

Pilate called together the chief priests and the rulers of the people; and he said unto them, Ye have brought this man unto me, as one that perverteth the people; and, behold, I, having examined him before you, have found no fault in him touching those things whereof ye accuse him: no, nor yet Herod.

Now, since at that feast the governor must of necessity release unto the people a prisoner, Pilate asked, Will ye that I release unto you Barabbas? or Jesus which is called the Christ?

They cried out all at once, Release Barabbas.

Pilate saith, What shall I do then with Jesus?

They cried out again, Let him be crucified.

Pilate saith, Shall I crucify your King?

The chief priests answered, We have no king but Caesar.

When Pilate saw that he could prevail nothing, he took water, and washed his hands before the multitude, saying, I am innocent of the blood of this just person: see ye to it.

Then answered the people, His blood be on us, and on our children.

And so Pilate, willing to content the people, gave sentence that it should be as they required. He released Barabbas; but he delivered Jesus, when he had scourged him, to their will, to be crucified.

Jesus is nailed to the cross

Matthew 27:27–38; Mark 15:16–27; Luke 23:26–34; John 19:17–20

The soldiers of the governor led Jesus into the common hall. They stripped him, and clothed him with purple; they plaited a crown of thorns, and put it about his head, and they put a reed in his right hand. Then they mocked him, saying, Hail, King of the Jews!

After that, they took off the purple from him, put his own raiment on him, smote him with their hands, and led him away to crucify him.

There followed a great company of people, many of them women, which bewailed him. But Jesus turning said,

Daughters of Jerusalem, weep not for me, but weep for yourselves, and for your children. For, behold, the days are coming, in the which they shall say, Blessed are the barren, and the wombs that never bare, and the paps which never gave suck.

Then shall they begin to say to the mountains,

Fall on us; and to the hills, Cover us.

  For if they do these things in a green tree, what shall be done in the dry?

And Jesus bearing his cross went forth.

As they came out, one Simon, a man of Cyrene, passed by, and on him they laid the cross, that he might bear it after Jesus.

When they were come to a place called the place of a skull, or, in Hebrew, Golgotha, they gave to Jesus wine mingled with myrrh: when he had tasted thereof, he would not drink. It was the third hour.

And there they crucified Jesus; him and the two malefactors: one on the right hand, and the other on the left, and Jesus in the midst.

Then said Jesus,

Father, forgive them; for they know not what they do.

Pilate wrote a title, and put it on the cross. It was written in Hebrew, Greek and Latin:

JESUS OF NAZARETH, THE KING OF THE JEWS.

Christ's words from the cross

Matthew 27:39–56; Mark 15:29–41; Luke 23:38–49; John 19:23–30

The soldiers, when they had crucified Jesus, took his garments, and cast lots upon them. The people that passed by derided him, wagging their heads, and saying, Ah, thou that destroy the temple and builds it in three days, save thyself!

The soldiers also mocked him, saying, If thou be the King of the Jews, save thyself!

Likewise the chief priests, mocking, said among themselves with the scribes, He saved others; himself he cannot save!

One of the two thieves which were crucified with him cast the same in his teeth; but the other rebuked him, saying, Dost thou not fear God? We receive the due reward of our deeds: but this man hath done nothing amiss.

And he said to Jesus, Lord, remember me when thou comest into thy kingdom.

Jesus said unto him,

Verily I say unto thee, today shalt thou be with me in paradise.

Now there stood by the cross Jesus's mother, his mother's sister, Mary the wife of Cleophas and Mary Magdalene. Jesus saw his mother, and he saw the disciple whom he loved standing by, and he said to his mother,

Woman, behold thy son!

Then he said to the disciple,

Behold thy mother!

And from that hour that disciple took her unto his own home. Now from the sixth hour there was darkness over all the land until the ninth hour. At the ninth hour Jesus cried with a loud voice, saying,

My God, my God, why hast thou forsaken me?

After this, Jesus, knowing that all things were now accomplished, said,

I thirst.

Straightway one of them ran and filled a sponge with vinegar, put it on a twig of hyssop, and put it to Jesus's mouth. When he had received the vinegar, he said,

It is finished.

And when he had cried again with a loud voice, he said,

Father, into thy hands I commend my spirit.

Having said thus, Jesus bowed his head, and yielded up the ghost.

All his acquaintance stood afar off, beholding these things.

Christ's body is laid in the tomb

Mark 15:42–47; Luke 23:50–56; John 19:38–42; Matthew 27:57–66

And when the even was come, Joseph of Arimathea went in unto Pilate and craved the body of Jesus.

A rich man of Arimathea, a city of the Jews, Joseph was an honourable counsellor, a good man, and a just (he had not consented to the counsel and deed of them). He also waited for the kingdom of God, being a disciple of Jesus, but secretly, for fear of the Jews.

This man went boldly in unto Pilate, and begged that he might take away the body of Jesus. Pilate gave him leave.

Joseph came, therefore, and took the body of Jesus. And there came also Nicodemus who brought a mixture of myrrh and aloes. Then took they the body, and wound it in a clean cloth of fine linen, with the spices, as the manner of the Jews is to bury.

Now in the place where Jesus was crucified there was a garden; and in the garden a new sepulchre, wherein was never man yet laid. And they laid the body in this, Joseph's own new tomb, which he had hewn out of the rock, and they rolled a great stone, nigh at hand, to the door of the sepulchre, and departed.

The women which came with Jesus from Galilee beheld the sepulchre, and how the body was laid.

Now the next day the chief priests and Pharisees came to Pilate saying, Sir, that deceiver said, while he was yet alive,

After three days I will rise again.

Command therefore that the sepulchre be made sure until the third day, lest his disciples come by night, and steal him away, and say unto the people, He is risen from the dead: so the last error shall be worse than the first.

Pilate said, Ye have a watch: make it as sure as you can. So they went and made the sepulchre sure, sealing the stone and setting a watch.

The resurrection

Matthew 28:1, 8–10; Mark 16:1–11; Luke 24:1–9; John 20:11–18

In the end of the sabbath, as it began to dawn toward the first day of the week, came Mary Magdalene and the other Mary, to see the sepulchre at the rising of the sun. They came bringing sweet spices that they might anoint him.

They said among themselves, Who shall roll away the stone from the door? and they found the stone rolled away.

They entered in, and found not the body of the Lord Jesus. And it came to pass, as they were perplexed, behold, two men stood by them in shining garments: they said, Why seek ye the living among the dead? he is not here: he is risen: remember how he spake when yet in Galilee, saying,

The Son of man must be delivered into the hands of sinful men, and be crucified, and the third day rise again.

They remembered his words, and they trembled, and went out quickly, with great joy; and did run to tell his disciples.

And, behold, Jesus met them, saying,

All hail!

And they worshipped him.
Then said Jesus unto them,

Be not afraid: go tell my brethren that they go into Galilee, and there shall they see me.

Mary Magdalene stood outside the sepulchre weeping: and she stooped and looked into the sepulchre and saw two angels in white, sitting.

They said, Why weepest thou?

She said, They have taken away my Lord.

When she had thus said, she turned, and saw Jesus standing, and knew not that it was Jesus.

He said,

Woman, why weepest thou? whom seekest thou?

She, supposing him to be the gardener, said, Sir, if thou have borne him hence, tell me where thou hast laid him, and I will take him away.

Jesus said,

Mary.

She turned, and said unto him, Master.
Jesus said unto her,

Touch me not; for I am not yet ascended to my Father: but go to my brethren, and say unto them, I ascend unto my Father, and your Father; and to my God, and your God.

Mary Magdalene came and told the disciples that she had seen the Lord, that he was alive, and that he had spoken these things unto her.

And they believed her not.

After the resurrection

Mark 16:12–13; Luke 24:13–31, 33–43; John 20:19-29

After that, Jesus appeared in another form unto two of them, that same day, as they walked to Emmaus, a village which was from Jerusalem about threescore furlongs.

While they talked together of all these things which had happened, Jesus himself drew near. But their eyes were holden that they should not know him. And he said unto them,

What manner of communications are these that ye have one to another, as ye walk, and are sad?

One of them, Cleopas, replied, Art thou a stranger in Jerusalem, and hast not known the things which are come to pass there in these days?

Jesus said,

What things?

They answered, Concerning Jesus of Nazareth: and how our

rulers have crucified him. But we trusted that it had been he which should have redeemed Israel.

Jesus said unto them,

O fools, and slow of heart to believe all that the prophets have spoken. Ought not Christ to have suffered these things, and to enter into his glory?

And beginning at Moses, he expounded the things in all the scriptures concerning himself.

They drew nigh unto the village whither they went: and Jesus made as if to go farther. But they constrained him, saying, Abide with us: for it is towards evening.

As he sat at meat with them, he took bread, and blessed it, and brake and gave to them. And their eyes were opened, and they knew him; and he vanished out of their sight.

The same hour, they returned to Jerusalem, and found the eleven gathered together, saying, The Lord is risen indeed, and hath appeared to Simon.

They told what things were done in the way, and how Jesus was known of them in the breaking of bread.

As they spake, with the doors shut for fear of the Jews, Jesus himself stood in the midst of them, and said,

Peace be unto you.

But they supposed they had seen a spirit, and were affrighted. And he said,

Why are ye troubled? and why do thoughts arise in your hearts? Behold my hands and my feet, that it is I myself: handle me, and see; for a spirit hath not flesh and bones, as ye see me have.

While they wondered, he said,

Have ye here any meat?

They gave him of a fish, and of a honeycomb; and he did eat before them.

Then said he to them again,

Peace be unto you; as my Father hath sent me, even so send I you.

Receive ye the Holy Ghost. Whosoever sins ye remit, they are remitted unto them: and whosoever sins ye retain, they are retained.

But Thomas was not with them when Jesus came. When the other disciples told him, We have seen the Lord, he said, Except I shall see in his hands the print of the nails, and put my finger into the print of the nails, and thrust my hand into his side, I will not believe.

After eight days, again the disciples were within, and Thomas with them: then came Jesus, as they sat at meat, the doors being shut, and stood in the midst, and said,

Peace be unto you.

Then saith he to Thomas,

Reach hither thy finger, and behold my hands; and reach hither thy hand, and thrust it into my side: and be not faithless, but believing.

Thomas answered, My Lord and my God.
Jesus said,

Thomas, because thou hast seen me, thou hast believed: blessed are they that have not seen, and yet have believed.

At the sea of Tiberias

John 21:1–23

Jesus showed himself again to the disciples at the sea of Tiberias; there were together Peter, and Thomas, and Nathanael, and the sons of Zebedee, and two others of his disciples.

Peter saith unto them, I am going to fish. They said, We go with thee. They entered into a ship immediately; and that night they caught nothing.

But when the morning was come, Jesus stood on the shore: but the disciples knew not that it was Jesus.

Then he asked them,

Children, have ye any meat?

They answered, No.
And he said,

Cast the net on the right side of the ship, and ye shall find.

They cast; and as soon as they were come to land, they saw a fire of coals there, and fish laid thereon, and bread.

Jesus said,

Bring of the fish which ye have now caught.

Peter drew the net to land full of great fishes: yet the net was not broken.

Jesus said to them,

Come and dine.

Jesus then taketh bread, and giveth them, and fish likewise. So when they had dined, Jesus said,

Simon, son of Jonas, lovest thou me more than these?

He replied, Yea, Lord; thou knowest that I love thee.

Jesus said,

Feed my lambs.

He said the second time,

Simon, son of Jonas, lovest thou me?

He said, Yea, Lord; thou knowest that I love thee.
Jesus said,

Feed my sheep.

He said the third time,

Simon, son of Jonas, lovest thou me?

Peter was grieved and said, Lord, thou knowest all things; thou knowest that I love thee.
Jesus said to him,

Feed my sheep. Verily, verily, I say unto thee, when thou wast young, thou girdedst thyself, and walkedst whither thou wouldest: but when thou shall be old, thou shalt stretch forth thy hands, and another shall gird thee, and carry thee whither thou wouldest not.

This spake he, signifying by what death he should glorify God. And he said to Peter,

Follow me.

Peter, turning about, saw the disciple whom Jesus loved following. Seeing him, Peter said, Lord, and what shall this man do?

Jesus answered,

If I will that he tarry till I come, what is that to thee? Follow thou me.

The ascension

Mark 16:14–18; Matthew 28:16–20; Luke 24:44–53; Acts 1:2–12

The eleven disciples went into a mountain in Galilee, where Jesus had appointed them. And he came, saying,

Go ye into all the world, and preach the gospel to every creature.

He that believeth and is baptized shall be saved; but he that believeth not shall be damned.

And these signs shall follow them that believe: In my name shall they cast out devils; they shall speak with new tongues; they shall take up serpents; and if they drink any deadly thing, it shall not hurt them; they shall lay hands on the sick, and they shall recover.

All power is given unto me in heaven and in earth. Go ye therefore, and teach all nations, baptizing them in the name of the Father, and of the Son, and of the Holy Ghost: teaching them to observe all things whatsoever I have commanded you: and, lo, I am with you always, even unto the end of the world.

And Jesus said unto them,

These are the words which I spake unto you while I was with you, that all things must be fulfilled, which were written in the law of Moses, and in the prophets, and in the psalms, concerning me.

Then opened he their understanding, that they might understand the scriptures. And he said unto them,

Thus it is written, and thus it behoved Christ to suffer, and to rise from the dead the third day: and that repentance and remission of sins should be preached in his name among all nations, beginning at Jerusalem.

And ye are witnesses of these things.

And, behold, I send the promise of my Father upon you: but tarry ye in the city of Jerusalem, until ye be endued with power from on high.

And it came to pass, while he blessed them, he was carried up into heaven; and a cloud received him out of their sight.

Then returned they with great joy unto Jerusalem, and they were continually in the temple praising and blessing God.

*

Thus the apostles to whom Jesus had chosen to show himself alive after his passion were commanded not to depart from Jerusalem:

Wait, tarry in Jerusalem, for the promise of the Father, which ye have heard of me. For John truly baptized with water; but ye shall be baptized with the Holy Ghost not many days hence.

They asked him, Lord, wilt thou at this time restore again the kingdom to Israel?

He said,

It is not for you to know the times or the seasons which the Father hath put in his own power. But ye shall receive power after that the Holy Ghost is come upon you: and ye shall be witnesses unto me both in Jerusalem, and in all Judea, and in Samaria, and unto the uttermost parts of the earth.

When he had spoken, while they beheld, he was taken up.

Saul's vision

Acts 8:3; 9:1–20

Saul made havoc of the church, entering into every house, and committing men and women to prison.

Breathing out threatenings against the disciples of the Lord, he went unto the high priest, and desired of him letters to the synagogues, that if he found any of them, whether men or women, he might bring them bound to Jerusalem.

As he journeyed, he came near Damascus: and suddenly there shone about him a light from heaven: and he fell to the earth, and heard a voice saying,

Saul, Saul, why persecutest thou me?

Saul said, Who art thou?
And the Lord said,

I am Jesus, whom thou persecutest: it is hard for thee to kick against the pricks.

Saul, trembling and astonished, said, Lord, what wilt thou have me to do?

The Lord answered,

Arise, and go into the city, and it shall be told thee what thou must do.

The men which journeyed with Saul stood speechless, hearing a voice, but seeing no man. Saul arose from the earth; and when his eyes were opened, he saw no man.

They led him by the hand into Damascus. And he was three days without sight, and neither did eat nor drink.

There was a certain disciple at Damascus, named Ananias; and to him said the Lord in a vision,

Ananias! Arise, and go into the street which is called Straight, and enquire in the house of Judas for one called Saul of Tarsus: for, behold, he prayeth, and hath seen in a vision a man named Ananias coming in, and putting his hand on him, that he might receive his sight.

Ananias answered, Lord, much evil hath he done to thy saints at Jerusalem.

But the Lord said,

Go thy way: for he is a chosen vessel unto me, to bear my name before the Gentiles, and kings, and the children of Israel: for I will show him how great things he must suffer for my name's sake.

Ananias entered the house; and, putting his hands on him, said, Brother Saul, the Lord, even Jesus, hath sent me, that thou might receive thy sight, and be filled with the Holy Ghost.

Immediately there fell from Saul's eyes as it had been scales; and he received sight forthwith, and arose, and was baptized.

Straightway Saul preached Christ in the synagogues, that he is the Son of God.

Simon Peter remembers

Acts 10:44–45; 11:16

While Peter spake, the Holy Ghost fell on all them which heard, They of the circumcision which believed were astonished, because on the Gentiles also was poured out the gift of the Holy Ghost.

Then remembered Peter how the Lord had said,

John indeed baptized with water; but ye shall be baptized with the Holy Ghost.

And he commanded them to be baptized.

Jesus's words to Paul in a vision

Acts 18:7–11

Paul entered into a certain man's house, a man named Justus who worshipped God and whose house joined hard to the synagogue.

Then spake the Lord to Paul in the night by a vision,

Be not afraid, but speak, and hold not thy peace;
for I am with thee, and no man shall set on thee to
hurt thee; for I have much people in this city.

And Paul continued there for a year and six months, teaching the word of God.

Paul's farewell to the Ephesians

Acts 20:17–19, 22, 25, 32–38

From Miletus, Paul sent to Ephesus and called the elders of the church. When they were come, he said unto them, Ye know, I have been with you at all times, serving the Lord with humility.

Now I go bound in the spirit unto Jerusalem, not knowing the things that shall befall me there. I know that ye shall see my face no more.

Brethren, I commend you to God.

I have coveted no man's silver, or gold, or apparel. I have showed you how ye ought to support the weak and to remember the words of the Lord Jesus, how he said,

It is more blessed to give than to receive.

When Paul had thus spoken, he prayed with them all. And they accompanied him unto the ship.

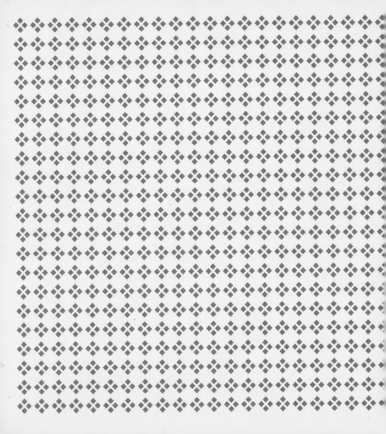